C000184682

Higher
BUSINESS MANAGEMENT

For SQA 2019 and beyond

Course Notes

Dr Lee Coutts

001/01042020

10 9 8 7 6 5 4 3 2 1

ISBN 9780008383473

Published by
Leckie & Leckie Ltd
An imprint of HarperCollins Publishers
Westerhill Road, Bishopbriggs, Glasgow, G64 2QT
T: 0844 576 8126   F: 0844 576 8131
leckiescotland@harpercollins.co.uk
www.leckiescotland.co.uk

Publisher: Sarah Mitchell
Project Managers: Janice McNeillie and Gillian Bowman

Special thanks to
Louise Robb (proofread)
Jess White (proofread)
Jouve (layout and illustrations)

Dedicated to the PGDE Business Education group of 2019/20 at the University of Strathclyde.

Printed and bound by CPI Group (UK) Ltd, Croydon CR0 4YY

A CIP Catalogue record for this book is available from the British Library.

Acknowledgements

We would like to thank the following for permission to reproduce their material:
P17 © Rose Carson/Shutterstock.com, P19 (police) © 1000 Words/Shutterstock.com, P20 © Martin Good/Shutterstock.com, P46 © Nick Beer/Shutterstock.com, P90 Tesco - This file is licensed under the Creative Commons Attribution 3.0 Unported license, P90 Poundland - This work is licensed under the Creative Commons Attribution-ShareAlike 3.0 License, P90 corner shop - This file is licensed under the Creative Commons Attribution 2.0 Generic license, P114 © Tupungato/Shutterstock.com, P133 MikeDotta/Shutterstock.com, P149 © PixieMe/Shutterstock.com

All other images from Shutterstock.

Text permissions

P25, Case study on H & M has been approved by and used with the kind permission of H & M; P31, Case study on Morrisons has been approved by and used with the kind permission of Morrisons Ltd; P31, Supermarket statistics chart with data provided by Kantar is used by permission; P114, Case study on FirstGroup Plc has been approved by and used with the kind permission of FirstGroup Plc.

Chapter 1

Welcome to Higher Business Management

Chapter 2

Understanding Business

Chapter 3

Management of Marketing

Chapter 4

Management of Operations

Chapter 5

Management of People

Chapter 6

Management of Finance

N.B. ALL topics within the Higher arrangements are included within this book. You will find topics, 'Technology in marketing', 'Technology in human resources' and 'Technology in finance' within the chapters, 'Management of marketing', 'Management of People' and 'Management of Finance' respectively. Topics have been covered in this way in order to allow students to make their own connections between the broader themes.

1 Welcome to Higher Business Management

What you will learn in this chapter:

- The structure of these Course Notes.
- The structure of Higher Business Management.
- The assessment of Higher Business Management.

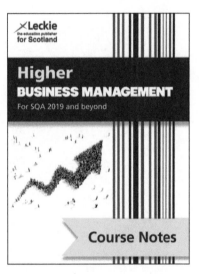

Introduction

These course notes have been written with learners in mind and support the teaching and learning of the Scottish Qualification Authority's (SQA) Higher Business Management course. These course notes have been significantly updated in 2019 to support the revised course.

The book has five chapters that each cover one area of study from the Higher Business Management course:

- Chapter 2 – Understanding Business
- Chapter 3 – Management of Marketing
- Chapter 4 – Management of Operations
- Chapter 5 – Management of People
- Chapter 6 – Management of Finance

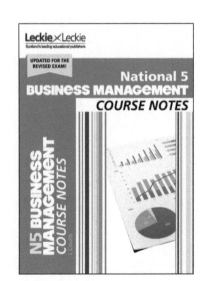

For those who have studied National 5 Business Management, these course notes will help consolidate and build on the knowledge and skills gained. For those who have not studied National 5 Business Management, it provides the knowledge and skills required to succeed in Higher Business Management. There are *revision activities* highlighted throughout this book that will help you revise key topics from National 5 or introduce these topics to you if you have not studied National 5 Business Management. If you have not studied National 5 Business Management, it is a good idea to obtain a copy of the Course Notes for it.

Higher Business Management covers topics not taught as part of the National 5 Business Management course, as well as building on existing topics, but also includes an emphasis on how large organisations operate, compared with small-to-medium-sized organisations at National 5.

Areas of study

Business is relevant to everybody, no matter what route their life is taking. We all come into contact with business on a daily basis, from using public transport to buying something in a shop or deciding to invest. Business has a powerful influence (positive and negative) on us, the economy and the world.

The five areas of study in Higher Business Management illustrate the different ways that large organisations operate. You will learn how people and societies depend on organisations to meet their needs and wants and how a range of factors influence and impact on how organisations operate.

Chapter 2 Understanding Business will develop your knowledge of large organisations in different sectors of the economy (private, public and third sector). You will learn about what factors (external and internal) impact on how organisations operate and the consequences of these factors. You will examine the different stakeholders that are interested in different organisations and how they are dependent on each other, as well as the ways they might come into conflict. Finally, you will examine the different ways organisations are structured and how decisions are made.

Chapter 3 Management of Marketing considers ways organisations try to satisfy their customers and how they can improve competitiveness. The extended marketing mix is covered (building on the marketing mix from National 5) and how technology enhances the marketing function is discussed.

Chapter 4 Management of Operations looks at the different ways organisations manage their production activities. Topics explored include managing inventory (stock), methods of production and ways of ensuring quality. The ethical and environmental issues arising from operations are explored, as is the role of technology in operations.

Chapter 5 Management of People considers the range of factors that organisations have to consider when managing people. Topics explored include workforce planning, training and development, motivating and leading people and managing employee relations. The legal implications of employing people are discussed and the role of technology in human resources is examined.

Chapter 6 Management of Finance examines how organisations manage finance. It discusses sources of finance for large organisations, cash budgeting and how to interpret and analyse the range of financial statements that large organisations produce. How technology can be used to assist the finance function is also considered.

> ⚠ **Watch point**
>
> Look for examples throughout these Course Notes of how technology can impact upon business activities.

Structure of these course notes

At the beginning of each chapter, you are reminded what topics are taught during National 5 Business Management and are told what you will learn in that specific chapter.

Throughout each chapter, there are different activities, quick questions, case studies and key questions to be answered.

- **Activities** allow you to apply knowledge in different situations. You might have to do some research, work in a group or prepare a presentation for your class. Each activity has a list of skills that will be developed.

- **Quick questions** test your knowledge of what you have learned.

- **Case studies** are real examples of large businesses. You should read the case study and answer the questions given. The case studies are very good preparation for your course assessment.

- **Key questions** will show you whether you have grasped the main points from each chapter. If you are required to do the unit assessments for Higher Business Management (your teacher or lecturer will advise you on this), key questions are an excellent source of revision.

At the end of each area of study, there are sample exam questions (with comments from an experienced examiner) and a traffic light self-assessment for you to complete.

There are also **watch points** throughout the book that provide you with specific pieces of advice to help your learning, and **make the link** that connects what you are learning to other parts of the course and/or other subjects. You can access the worksheets for the **revision activities at https://collins.co.uk/pages/scottish-curriculum-free-resources.**

Course assessment

Your teacher/lecturer will provide you with feedback regularly to let you know how well you are learning the topics in the course. You will also have the opportunity to get feedback from your peers and to reflect on your own learning.

Higher Business Management is certificated by the Scottish Qualifications Authority (SQA) and the course assessment gives you an overall mark that determines the grade that you will be awarded (A, B, C, D or No Award). The course assessment allows you to demonstrate that you have achieved the aims of the course and to show you can:

- draw on the knowledge and skills gained throughout the course

- show in-depth knowledge and skills in different topics

- apply the knowledge and skills you have learned in different contexts.

The course assessment for Higher Business Management consists of two parts (a question paper and an assignment) and is out of 120 marks.

Question paper	The question paper contributes 75% of the marks towards the overall course grade. You will have 2 hours and 45 minutes to sit the question paper. The question paper is undertaken under examination conditions and you will not know in advance what topics will be assessed.
The question paper is allocated 90 marks and contributes 75% towards the grade for the course.	The question paper contains two sections. Section 1 contains one question (broken down into different parts) based on a case study. Section 1 is worth 30 marks. Section 2 is worth 60 marks and contains four questions each worth 15 marks.
Assignment	The assignment will require you to undertake research on an organisation of your choice and to present your findings as a business report. You will have to show that you can research, analyse, evaluate and make decisions. It is designed to be challenging and to get you really thinking about what you have learned. The assignment has to be completed under conditions stipulated by SQA.
The assignment is allocated 30 marks and contributes 25% towards the grade for the course.	

⚠ Watch point

Use past examination papers from the SQA's website to become familiar with the structure and format of the question paper.

Skills for learning, life and work

Higher Business Management allows you to develop broad, generic skills that are needed in learning, life and work. The skills developed in this course are:

⚠ Watch point

Every activity in these course notes contain a list of the skills for learning, life and work you are developing.

Literacy (Writing)	This involves writing text that presents information, ideas and opinions on a topic. Your assignment will require you to show that you can do this.
Numeracy (Information handling)	This requires you being able to interpret and analyse graphs, data in tables and in other forms. It also requires you to think about the reliability of the information presented.
Employability, enterprise and citizenship (Employability and enterprise)	Employability allows you to develop the skills, qualities, attributes and knowledge required for work. Enterprise involves you having the ability to take risk and manage change. It encourages you to be creative and innovative and to assess risk before making decisions.
Thinking skills (Applying and analysing & evaluating)	Applying requires you to use existing information to help in solving problems. It also requires you to use information in different contexts and when planning a task. Analysing and evaluating involves thinking about a situation or scenario, and considering the benefits and costs of each one to help reach a conclusion.

GO! Individual activity

You might want to keep a learning journal throughout the Business Management course.

This journal is not part of course assessment, but will get you thinking about your learning and is a place where you can keep different things that you have learned. It will help you to develop different skills, as well as to improve your knowledge of Business Management. At this level, it is crucial that you are able to carry out your own research, evaluate different sources of information and use business terminology correctly. Your learning journal will help you do this.

Your learning journal could take a number of formats and you can decide how you want it to look. You might simply use a jotter to record things and stick things into or you might have a folder that you could use. You could also keep an online blog or portfolio.

To get started you should:

- Decide what format your learning journal will take – will it be a jotter, a folder or electronic (e.g. using a blog or online journal)?
- Start your learning journal by creating a front cover or setting up your blog/journal ready to write in.

Answer the following questions at the beginning of your learning journal:

1. Why have you chosen the format for your journal that you did?

2. What do you want to get from studying Higher Business Management?

3. How will you try to achieve what you want to get from the course?

4. What extra demand will Higher place on you compared to National 5?

Remember, your learning journal is a record of your learning journey throughout this course. This book contains prompts to remind you to record things, but you should feel free to write as much as you can about your learning in Business Management. Your teacher/ lecturer might want to see it on a regular basis to make sure you are keeping it up-to-date and professional.

Skills

- Writing
- Employability
- Applying
- Analysing & evaluating

2 Understanding Business

The role of business in society

> **⚠ Watch point**
>
> Needs are essential for survival (e.g. water, shelter) whereas wants are desired items (e.g. mobile phone, car).

Businesses aim to satisfy the needs and wants of their customers, by providing goods and services, in a competitive environment.

Sectors of industry

Primary

Businesses in the primary sector extract raw materials from the ground. These businesses include agriculture, fishing, oil and gas extraction, and mining.

Secondary

Businesses in this sector manufacture goods. They take raw materials and transform them into a tangible, finished product. Examples include shipbuilding, breweries and builders.

Tertiary

Businesses in the tertiary sector provide a service, an intangible product. The service is provided by people who have been trained to offer it. Examples include fitness instructors, hotels, supermarkets, hairdressers and health care providers.

Quaternary

This is the newest sector of industry. Businesses in the quaternary sector provide a knowledge-based and information service and are often concerned with innovation, research and development. This includes consultancy, ICT and computing, education, scientific research and financial services. People working in the quaternary sector are highly skilled.

Trends

Each country tends to move from one sector to the next after a period of time; the United Kingdom is a good example. In industrialised countries, the tertiary and quaternary sectors now account for most of the business activity that takes place. Primary and secondary industries no longer have such a major role in these countries but there is still some evidence of these activities taking place, even in Scotland. For example, a significant amount of oil and gas extraction still takes place off the coast of Aberdeen and shipbuilding still takes place on the Clyde in Glasgow.

⚠ Watch point

Businesses can belong to more than one sector of industry.

GO! Paired activity

Do some research to find out:

1. The proportion of businesses in each sector of industry in the UK today.
2. Reasons why the UK has moved from one sector to another.

Present your results in a poster and include a graph showing your answer to Q1. Make sure your graph is labelled appropriately. For Q2, try to analyse and interpret as best you can the reasons you find. Your Teacher/Lecturer will help you with this.

Y Skills

- Information handling
- Employability
- Applying
- Analysing & evaluating

Wealth creation

Wealth is created by a business by **adding value** to a product as it goes through the production process. Let's recap this process from National 5; when jeans are being made, they go through the following chain of production:

Cotton is cleaned thoroughly

↓

Indigo is used to turn the cotton blue

↓

The cotton is weaved together into denim

↓

Parts of the jeans are cut out of the denim using templates

↓

Workers sew the parts of the jeans together

↓

The jeans are stone washed to make them look worn

↓

The jeans are pressed

As the jeans move from one stage of production to another, **wealth is being created**.

This is because **value is being added** to the price that will be charged by the business for the product.

Think about it … the jeans are worth more as a finished product rather than all the raw materials (cotton, indigo, buttons, zip etc) sitting in a pile themselves. Another example would be building a house; as the house is built it is worth more than the bricks, wood and paint sitting on an empty piece of land doing nothing.

When we add up the final value of all goods and services provided in the UK, we have a figure known as the **gross domestic product (GDP)**. At Higher level, we need to consider the impact that the process of creating wealth has on the UK economy.

Benefits of creating wealth	Costs of creating wealth
• Jobs are created and therefore this reduces the UK's unemployment figure • When people become employed, they might have access to training and the opportunity to learn new skills • As a result of less unemployment, demand for goods and services increases and the standard of living increases • Tax is paid by businesses and individuals when they have a job and this money is paid to the Government who can then invest this money into different Government services, e.g. health, police and education • Other businesses will be keen to invest • Infrastructure (e.g. access to utilities such as water and electricity) can be improved, as can roads and transport links	• Businesses can have a large environmental impact on a country or specific location (e.g. noise and traffic pollution and an increase in wastage) • The volume of non-renewable resources, e.g. oil, can decrease • Greenfield sites (land that has previously been unused or used for agriculture) are lost – however, this could be seen as an advantage • Too much demand for goods and services can cause inflation; this is when the price of goods and services rises and may mean people can no longer afford to purchase some products

GO! Group activity

Think of a project happening in your local area (e.g. a new business being built). Prepare a brief presentation on this project. Your presentation should include:

1. A brief introduction to the project you have chosen and why.
2. Some background information on the project.
3. Why the project is taking place.
4. The benefits of the project to the economy and environment.
5. The costs of the project to the economy and environment.
6. A conclusion, with reasons, stating why your group thinks the project will benefit the local area or not.

Be prepared to evaluate your presentation once you have delivered it. Note down any improvements you could make next time in your learning journal, and what you could have done to improve your own contribution.

Skills

* Writing
* Applying
* Analysing & evaluating

Make the link

Environmental issues are explored in various chapters in these Course Notes.

⚠ Watch point

Keep up-to-date with what is happening in the economy in the TV/radio news and in good quality newspapers. Ask your Teacher/Lecturer for more information about the features of good quality newspapers.

🔵 Individual activity

The Commonwealth Games took place in Glasgow in 2014. This had a positive and negative impact on Glasgow and, in particular, the specific locations in which events took place. Your task is to do some research and find out:

1. The number of jobs the Games created, both during construction and while the games took place, and the benefits of this job creation.
2. The facilities that the Games have provided for the people of Glasgow and the benefits of these new facilities.
3. The number of people who visited Glasgow for the Games and the benefits of this on the local economy.
4. Examples of the negative impact the Games have had on the local community and Glasgow, and the extent of that impact.

When you are completing this task, really try to think about (analyse) the consequences of what you are finding out. Be prepared to discuss your findings with the rest of your class. Your Teacher/Lecturer will collate a detailed analysis of all the findings of the class.

🌱 Skills

- Applying
- Analysing & evaluating

❓Questions

1. Describe the four sectors of industry.
2. Define the term 'wealth creation'.
3. Define the term 'gross domestic product'.
4. Suggest three benefits and three costs of creating wealth for the UK.

Types of business organisations

A business belongs to one sector of the economy. At National 5, the focus was on small-to-medium-sized organisations, whereas at Higher, the focus is on large organisations. A large organisation is one that employs more than 250 people.

Organisations in the private sector have the primary aim to make profit. Organisations in the public sector aim to provide a service, and those in the third sector aim to support a specific cause.

💡 Make the link

Make sure you revise what you learned at National 5 about types of businesses.

💡 Revision Activity

Download and complete the revision sheet from the Leckie & Leckie website. This looks at types of businesses.

At National 5, the following types of businesses were explored:

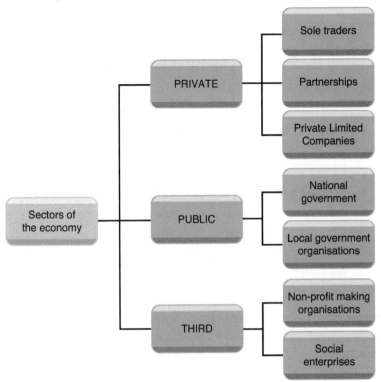

Private sector

Private sector organisations are owned by individuals and aim to make a profit.

	Sole trader	Partnership	Private Limited Company
What is it?	A business owned by one person.	A business owned by 2–20 people.	A company owned by people who have been invited to buy shares.
Who owns it?	The sole trader	The partners	The shareholders
Who controls it?	The sole trader	The partners	Board of Directors
Examples	Rob Jackson Joinery	Adams & McNeill Accountants	Fly High Travel Ltd

Sole traders are usually small businesses and are a popular choice when people are starting up a business. Normally the sole trader would invest his or her own money (this is known as capital) into the business when starting it up.

The benefits of being a sole trader are:

- Easy to set up; do not need to complete lots of legal documents.

- All of the profits are kept by the owner.

⚠ Watch point

A good way to remember the features of different types of business is to think about who owns and who controls it.

- The owner can choose when to work and when to take holidays.

- All the decisions are made by the owner and can be made quickly without having to consult other people.

The costs of being a sole trader are:

- There is nobody to share the workload and responsibility with.

- Raising large amounts of start-up capital can be difficult as the business might be seen as more of a risk compared to a larger, more established business.

- Unlimited liability – this means if the business fails, the sole trader is personally responsible for any debts.

- It can be difficult to obtain economy of scale, which is one of the benefits of being a big business, e.g. discounts for bulk-buying.

Partnerships are usually small-to-medium-sized businesses. Each partner brings a share of capital to the business when it is starting up.

The benefits of a partnership are:

- Workload, responsibility and decision making can be shared amongst the partners – it isn't down to one person.

- Different partners often bring different experiences and skills.

- Finance can be raised more easily compared to a sole trader.

- Customers and suppliers might see a partnership as being less of a risk to deal with compared to a sole trader.

The costs of a partnership are:

- Any profit that the business makes is split between partners.

- Unlimited liability for each partner.

- Arguments between partners might happen and could slow down decision making.

- A legal document known as a partnership agreement needs to be created. The partnership agreement sets out how profits will be split.

Private Limited Companies usually have the letters 'Ltd' after their name, but not always, so recognising one can sometimes be difficult.

To be an owner of a Ltd company you have to buy shares. These shares are not available to just anyone and normally you would be invited to buy them from people who are already connected to the business, such as family or friends. Normally shareholders would receive a return on the money they have invested in the business called a **dividend**. Even though shareholders own it, the responsibility for running the business is delegated (which simply means given to) a Board of Directors who have the job of managing the company.

When a Ltd company is being set up, legal documents have to be created and sent to an organisation called **Companies House**, where a copy is kept. These documents are called a **Memorandum of Association** and **Articles of Association** and contain detailed information about how the business will operate.

The benefits of a Ltd company are:

- Limited liability for shareholders – unlike sole traders and partnerships, if the business fails, shareholders only lose the money they have invested into the company when buying shares. Their own personal possessions (e.g. a house) would not be sold to pay off the business debts.

- Finance can be raised by selling more shares to existing shareholders or inviting new people to buy.

- Shareholders and Directors can bring different experience and skills.

The costs of a Ltd company are:

- More complicated to set up compared to a sole trader or partnership because of the legal process involved.

- The rules laid down by the law – The Companies Act – have to be followed.

- Each year, financial accounts showing the financial position of the company have to be published.

- The cost of setting up a Ltd company can be high.

At Higher level, you need to be able to compare the features of different large organisations from the following three sectors of the economy:

Private Sector	Public Sector	Third Sector
• Public limited companies • Franchises • Multinationals	• National government organisations and agencies	• Non-profit making organisations, e.g. charities • Social enterprises

⚠ Watch point

Sectors of the economy (public, private, third) are different from sectors of industry (primary, secondary, tertiary, quaternary).

⚠ Watch point

When comparing different types of businesses, think about: who owns them, who controls them and how they are financed.

Public limited companies

A public limited company (plc) is a company that is owned by shareholders. Shareholders are people who have bought shares in the company, perhaps through the London Stock Exchange. The company is owned by shareholders and run by a Board of Directors who have been appointed on behalf of shareholders to control and manage the company.

Benefits

- Limited liability for the shareholders of the company (this means if the company was to go bankrupt, shareholders would only lose the money they invested into the company and not their own personal assets). This also means that shareholders are maybe more likely to invest in the company.

- Large amounts of capital (finance) can be raised by selling more shares via the stock exchange and lenders may feel more confident in investing in larger companies.

- Can often take advantage of economies of scale because of their size. This means they can obtain discounts for buying, e.g. raw materials in bulk.

- Plcs can control more of the market compared to smaller organisations and therefore have more power within it.

Costs

- Financial statements have to be published annually, which will involve a cost to produce them.

- There is no control over who can buy shares in the company.

- The company has to abide by the Companies Act to avoid legal action being taken.

- Profits may be lower when the company is initially set up due to high start-up costs.

Franchises

Ever fancied having your own McDonald's restaurant? Well, you can, by opening a franchise. A person who starts a business and provides a product or service supplied by another business (the **franchisor**) is known as a **franchisee** and operates a business known as a **franchise**. The franchisee is allowed to use the business name (e.g. McDonald's) and sell its products.

There are benefits and costs of franchising to both the **franchisee** and **franchisor**.

Franchisee:

Benefits	Costs
• They can set up a business using a business name that is well established and that people are familiar with. This could allow them to gain customers and sales quickly compared to setting up a brand new business. It also reduces the risk of failure. • Advertising costs are paid for by the franchisor, which saves the franchisee having to spend money on this themselves. • Franchisor carries out training for the whole business and therefore it is appropriate to the needs of the workforce and will save the franchisee money.	• It requires a considerable sum of money to set up a franchise and the franchisee may not have this money available. • The franchisee might have little or no control over the products available, their price or the layout of the store. The franchisee might find this frustrating as they cannot inject any new ideas into the business. • Some of the profit earned has to be given to the franchisor, thereby reducing the money that the franchisee earns.

Franchisor:

Benefits	Costs
• Income is guaranteed as the franchisee normally pays a percentage of profit each year to the franchisor. • If the business does not work, the cost of failure is split and therefore risk is shared. • Market share of the whole franchise increases as more branches are being opened.	• As only a percentage of turnover is given to the franchisor by the franchisee, this might be lower than what the franchisor could have earned themselves. • A franchisee could damage the reputation and image of the business and this could cause problems for the whole franchise.

Multinationals

A multinational organisation is one that operates in more than one country. It will normally have a headquarters based in one country; this is known as the 'home' country. Because it operates in more than one country, it will be globally recognised. A socially responsible multinational organisation may have a positive impact on the local economy and community by providing jobs and creating wealth for the local area.

Benefits

- Economies of scale can be taken advantage of, therefore reducing costs.

- Legal restrictions can be avoided in other countries compared to the home country.

- May be able to take advantage of different tax regulations in other countries, therefore increasing profitability.

- Expanding abroad will mean the organisation becomes bigger, increasing sales, and also safer from takeovers by other organisations.

- Government grants that do not require to be paid back might be given in some countries for locating there.

- Resources, e.g. labour, might be cheaper in some countries, reducing the overall expenses.

Costs

- Each country's laws need to be complied with, which might mean changes need to be made to the goods or service, and these might be expensive.

- The culture might vary from one country to another and the organisation will need to consider this.

- Language barriers may make trading more difficult and expensive if language interpreters need to be employed.

- Language barriers may also mean that communication is misinterpreted and decisions wrongly made.

Public sector

Public sector organisations are owned by the Government on behalf of the taxpayer and aim to provide a service to the general public. They are funded by taxes that individuals and businesses have to pay. Different types of taxes exist including income tax, sugar tax, road tax and council tax.

> ### 🔵 Individual activity
>
> Do some research to find out the purpose of the following Government agencies:
>
> - HM Revenue & Customs
>
> - Royal Mint
>
> - Financial Conduct Authority

Scottish Government

The Scottish Government has delegated responsibility from the UK Parliament for issues such as education, health, transport, law and order, housing, rural affairs, tourism and some aspects of taxation. It is run by Members of the Scottish Parliament (MSPs), who are elected by the Scottish public.

Local government organisations

Local government organisations (or local authorities) get funding from the Scottish Government to deliver specific services in a specific area of Scotland. These include running schools, providing leisure facilities and emptying our rubbish bins!

> ### 🔵 Paired activity
>
> Using the Scottish Government's website, research the following:
>
> 1) The difference between the Scottish Government and the Scottish Parliament.
>
> 2) The responsibilities of the First Minister.
>
> 3) The difference between the Scottish Cabinet and Ministers.
>
> 4) The main aim of the current Programme for Government.
>
> ### Skills
>
> - Applying

Third sector

Non-profit making organisations such as charities and voluntary organisations are set up to support specific causes.

Charities are owned and controlled by a Board of Trustees. They are regulated by the Government, and the income they make is put towards a specific cause. Charities will undertake fundraising activities to raise finance, e.g. by asking for grants/donations through TV appeals, street collections or by selling unwanted items in a charity shop.

Voluntary organisations such as community football clubs or youth clubs aim to provide a service to people, but without the profit-making motive. A committee is normally set up to manage the voluntary organisation and people will volunteer to undertake specific duties, e.g. Chairperson, Secretary etc. Most voluntary organisations will ask for donations as well as holding fundraising events, e.g. fun days and sponsored events, to raise finance.

Social enterprises

Social enterprises trade in all markets, selling goods and services to individual consumers, local authorities, government and private businesses. Social enterprises have a social or environmental aim rather than to make profit for owners or shareholders, but are run in a business-like way. The business will let customers know what the social enterprise is trying to do and who it is trying to help. All of the profit that it makes, through selling goods and services, must be invested into meeting the aim of the social enterprise. Unlike some charities, they don't rely on grants and donations, but some social enterprises do become charities. The main difference between a social enterprise and a charity is its legal structure and the fact that social enterprises have less regulation by the Government. Social enterprises can attract customers and employees who want to help the cause.

Examples of social enterprises

- **Aberdeen Foyer** – a social enterprise set up to try and help homeless youths in the Aberdeenshire area. As well as this, they provide opportunities for young people to develop employability and life skills. The opportunities they provide range from construction and property maintenance to graphic design and driving training.

- **Active4All** – this social enterprise provides nearly 100 jobs by collecting waste materials and unwanted furniture and then selling them. It is based in Glasgow.

- **MissMsMrs** – a social enterprise with the aim of empowering girls and women, by increasing their self-esteem and developing their self-care.

> ⚠ **Watch point**
>
> A social enterprise is different from a private sector business that operates in an ethical or socially responsible way.

🔵GO! Class activity

Arrange a visit to a local social enterprise or invite a speaker from a local social enterprise along to talk to your class.
Try to find out as much as you can about how the social enterprise works, what it does and the benefits that it brings.

Skills

- Enterprise
- Applying

🔵GO! Group activity

Use online maps (e.g. Google Maps) to examine the number of private, public and third-sector businesses in your local area.

Skills

- Applying

🔵GO! Further reading

Further information on social enterprises can be found by using the following websites:
Social Enterprise Scotland –
http://www.socialenterprisescotland.org.uk/
Just Enterprise – http://www.justenterprise.org/
Social Enterprise UK – http://www.socialenterprise.org.uk/
Glasgow Social Enterprise Network –
https://www.gsen.org.uk/

GO! Individual activity

Create a table to compare different types of businesses (private limited companies, public limited companies, franchises, multinationals, public sector organisations and third sector organisations) in terms of:

- who owns them
- who controls them
- how they are financed
- benefits
- costs.

Skills

- Applying
- Analysing & evaluating

? Questions

1. Compare a private limited company and a public limited company.
2. Describe two benefits and two costs of a public limited company.
3. Define the term 'franchise'.
4. Suggest two benefits and two costs of franchising for the franchisor.
5. Suggest two benefits and two costs of franchising for the franchisee.
6. Suggest two benefits and two costs of being a multinational.
7. Suggest how a multinational may be socially responsible.
8. What impact might the following have for a multinational?
   - Language differences
   - Cultural differences
   - Cheaper labour
   - Different tax rates
   - Easier access to raw materials
9. Compare local and national government.
10. Describe the different organisations operating in the third sector.
11. Distinguish between a public limited company and public sector organisation in terms of ownership and control.

Objectives

An **objective** is a goal or a target that a business has. They provide a focus for the organisation and its workforce to work towards over a period of time. They are important because they can be used to measure how successful an organisation is. An organisation will usually make its objectives public, e.g. in its mission statement and on its website.

A **mission statement** sets out the vision and aims of an organisation. It lets different stakeholders see what the organisation will do in the future and what it might mean for them:

> ### ⚠ Watch point
> Different types of businesses will have different objectives.

- It will tell employees what it plans to do and they can think about how this would impact their own job.

- Prospective employees might use it to see whether their own values match those of the organisation and whether or not they would fit in.

- It can be used to inform customers about future plans the organisation has.

- It can be used to raise the profile and image of the organisation and might attract media attention and, in the long run, potentially increase sales.

A number of objectives were explored at National 5. However, at Higher level, it is necessary to be able to justify why an objective is important, as well as learning about other objectives.

Objective	What is it?	Why is it important?
Survival	To continue trading; to exist.	Other objectives would be pointless if the business did not exist.
Profit	To have more income (e.g. through sales) than costs.	Most private sector businesses have this aim. Dividend payments to shareholders in a plc will be based on profit.
Customer Satisfaction	To make customers happy.	To ensure customer loyalty and to encourage new customers.
Market Leader	To become the biggest business in a market.	This will highlight the fact that the business has the greatest number of customers compared to competitors.

Other objectives that we need to learn about at Higher are:

- Corporate social responsibility

- Satisficing

> ### ⚠ Watch point
> Make sure you can say why an objective is important for a business.

- Managerial objectives
- Growth

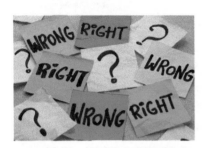

Corporate social responsibility

Corporate social responsibility (CSR) might be known as social responsibility or ethics. An organisation with this aim will behave in a responsible way; this might involve treating suppliers fairly and/or protecting the environment. Large organisations may have a code of conduct or a set of regulations that must be complied with if working with that organisation (e.g. a code of conduct on what it expects from its suppliers).

There are many different ways an organisation can be socially responsible:

- Making sure raw materials come from sustainable sources (sources that can be replaced), e.g. trees when paper is being manufactured (see page 112).

- Trying to reduce its carbon footprint as much as possible, e.g. using the most environmentally friendly method of distribution (see page 112).

- Making sure suppliers are paid fairly for what they produce, e.g. by adopting a fair trade policy (see page 112).

- Recycling as much as possible and reducing waste going to landfill (see page 111).

- Providing opportunities for employees to participate in physical activity and promoting healthy eating, e.g. providing cycling facilities to get to work or providing healthy options in the canteen.

- Reducing water and energy wastage.

- Reducing the amount of plastic being used in packaging.

- Using electric vehicles.

Make the link

Fair trade (page 112) is also relevant when exploring social responsibility.

This objective is becoming more important in a modern world; people expect businesses to behave responsibly and, if they don't, this will impact negatively on their image and customers would likely shop elsewhere. While acting in a socially responsible way might be costly in the short-term for an organisation, the long-term benefits of adopting this aim will far outweigh the costs and potential consequences of not doing so!

H&M Case Study

H&M is a fashion business that forms part of the H&M Group plc. It offers a range of fashion products and accessories for every season and style. It was formed in 1947 in Sweden and currently has 4,492 stores across the world. It has a long-term aim of expansion both online and in stores.

H&M is committed to social responsibility and operating in a sustainable and ethical way. Its commitment to this is embedded within its culture and values. It considers both current and future generations in the way it plans its ambitions and goals.

H&M has 3 key ambitions:

100% leading the change

100% fair & equal

100% circular & climate positive

It aims to drive innovation, promote transparency and praise sustainable activities (for example. through large orders to suppliers) as part of its ambition of achieving 100% Leading the Change. As part of its 100% Circular & Climate Positive ambition, it believes in a circular approach to the production and use of products (that is, a circular lifecycle rather than one that simply ends) and is committed to using only recycled or raw materials that are sustainably sourced by 2030. Finally, H&M is committed to being 100% Fair & Equal by providing fair jobs for everyone and valuing inclusion and diversity. They have a belief that all employees should be respected, treated fairly and work in a safe and healthy environment. For example, employees of suppliers must work in safe buildings and not be exposed to hazardous equipment or conditions. H&M have a Sustainability Commitment (previously a Code of Conduct), that sets out the standards expected of any supplier or organisation working with H&M.

Source: https://sustainability.hm.com/

Questions

1. Define the term social responsibility.
2. What does H&M's Sustainability Commitment replace?
3. What does H&M's Sustainability Commitment set out?
4. Give an example of what action H&M is taking to achieve each of its 3 ambitions.
5. Explain two consequences for H&M of not operating in a socially responsible way.

Paired activity

You are going to find out more about an organisation and its commitment to social responsibility.

1. Choose an organisation.
2. Do some research to find out about its commitment to social responsibility.

   - What does its mission statement say about social responsibility?
   - Does it have a policy or code of conduct?
   - What does it expect of its stakeholders?
   - What does it do to behave ethically?
   - How does it make sure that social responsibility is being implemented?

Summarise your findings in a poster, short presentation or in a discussion forum. Be prepared to share these with the rest of your class.

Skills

- Writing
- Applying
- Analysing & evaluating

Group or class discussion

Find some examples of an organisation that has been criticised in the media for not being socially responsible.

- What did the organisation do?
- What consequences or possible consequences has it had for the organisation?
- What recommendations do you have for the organisation to avoid this situation in the future?
- What would the costs and benefits of these recommendations be?

Summarise your findings in a poster, short presentation or in a discussion forum. Be prepared to share these with the rest of your class.

Skills

- Writing
- Applying
- Analysing & evaluating

Satisficing

This means aiming for a satisfactory position, i.e. 'it is good enough'. It is based on the idea of Herbert Simon, a famous economist. It might not be the ideal situation or solution but it will be adequate. Sometimes it is not possible to aim for the ideal situation or solution, particularly in the short-term, because of the costs involved or because of external factors (e.g. an uncertain economy or legislation) that might prevent the ideal being achieved.

Make the link

External factors are covered on pages 33–40.

Managerial objectives

Managers might have their own internal objectives. They might want to receive bonuses for achieving certain targets or other fringe benefits ('perks') such as a company car. These objectives can be motivating to a manager but they might put their own objectives before the organisation's.

Growth

Businesses might aim to grow for a number of reasons:

- To increase sales and profit, which in turn will increase the return on investment for owners (e.g. dividends for shareholders).

- To increase the number of customers, which will increase profits and market share, and may enable the organisation to become a marker leader.

- To take advantage of economies of scale (discounts for bulk buying), thereby reducing costs.

- To reduce the risk of a takeover by another organisation.

- To gain a better reputation in the marketplace, which will encourage new customers to buy, thereby increasing sales and ultimately profit.

Businesses can grow in a number of ways. The diagram below shows you some of the different methods of growth.

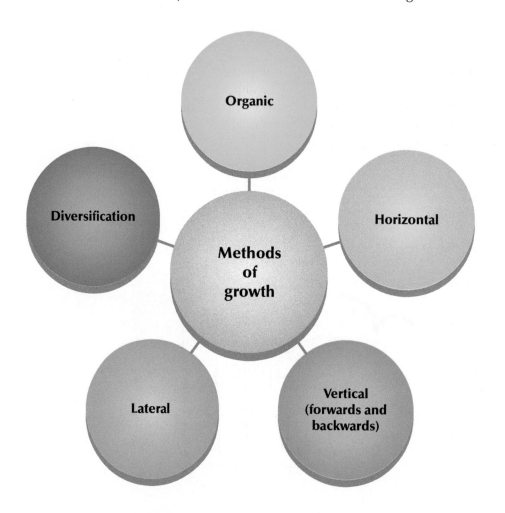

Methods of growth

Organic growth

Organic (or internal) growth happens when the business increases the number of goods and services it offers or increases the number of branches/outlets and employees that it has. Increasing the number of branches or outlets a business has may mean they can attract new customers in new locations. The business may also decide to begin selling online to target customers 24/7 or increase output by increasing production capacity (e.g. expanding a factory or adopting technology that allows more to be produced). Growing organically allows the business to retain control over its activities (compared with, for example, merging with another).

Horizontal growth

Horizontal growth occurs when two businesses providing the same service, or producing the same product, join together (e.g. two airlines joining together). This will cause the business to become bigger and gain a greater market share, and will reduce the number of competitors in the market. As a result of fewer competitors, higher prices could be charged by the business. It also allows the business to gain economies of scale, which will in turn lower production costs and increase profit.

Vertical growth

When businesses in the same industry, but who operate at different stages of production, join together this is called vertical growth. This cuts out the middlemen involved with two separate businesses, and therefore cuts costs. There are two forms of vertical growth:

- **Backward vertical** – taking over a supplier, e.g. a jeans manufacturer taking over a cotton farmer. By taking over a supplier it means that the business should have sufficient supplies available at reasonable prices, as they will not need to add the element of profit to raw materials. As the business now has control over inputs, quality can be more readily assured. They may also be able to limit the supply of input inventory being supplied to competitors.

- **Forward vertical** – taking over a customer, e.g. a jeans manufacturer taking over a jeans shop. By taking over a customer this will mean that supplies are readily available to the shop, helping to ensure regular sales. It would allow, in this example, the manufacturer to have control over the level of customer service given to the customer, rather than it being provided by another business.

Lateral growth

When two businesses who are in different, but related, industries come together this is known as lateral growth. For example, an airline and a ferry company.

Diversification

Diversification is when two businesses that provide different goods and services join together. It is also referred to as a conglomerate. It will reduce the risk of failure by operating in more than one market and will also allow profit to be obtained from more than one market. Diversification can also occur when one business decides to begin trading in a new market, e.g. a supermarket deciding to open an optician or pharmacy. This also reduces risk and allows for increased profits.

Ways to achieve growth

Developing products, increased promotion and increasing staffing can achieve growth. Growth can also be achieved by franchising or becoming a multinational (as discussed earlier in this chapter). However, a business can also grow by taking over another or by merging with another business:

- A **takeover** is when one large business takes control and ownership of a smaller business.

- A **merger** is when two businesses of approximately the same size agree to become one. This will allow sales and market share to increase.

GO! Individual activity

For each type of business provided below, describe one objective it may have and the reason why. Provide a different objective for each type of business.

- Private limited company
- Public limited company
- Multinational
- Franchise
- NHS Scotland
- Glasgow City Council
- A charity
- A social enterprise

Skills

- Applying
- Analysing & evaluating

🔍 Case study

Morrisons

Morrisons began as a market stall in Bradford, England, and is now one of the UK's biggest supermarket chains. It currently has a 9.9% share of the supermarket market. It employs over 100,000 people in its supermarkets as well as in other parts of its business. It has over 150,000 trolleys in its supermarkets!

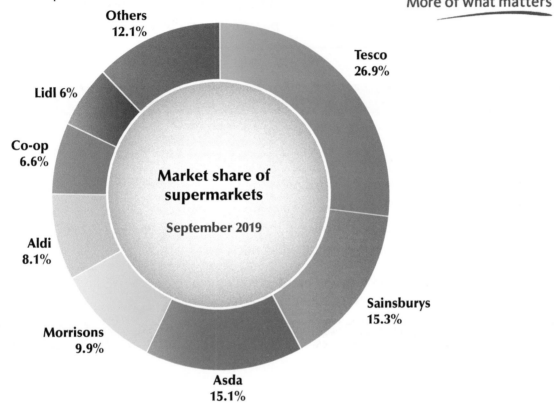

Others 12.1%

Tesco 26.9%

Lidl 6%

Co-op 6.6%

Market share of supermarkets

September 2019

Aldi 8.1%

Sainsburys 15.3%

Morrisons 9.9%

Asda 15.1%

Source: Kantar

The source of Morrisons' food has always been a key concern. Morrisons is unusual because it is 'vertically integrated'. As well as sourcing food from suppliers, it makes more than half the fresh food it sells in its foodmaking sites. This enables it to control cost and quality and cut out the middleman. Morrisons has a clear commitment to social responsibility. It is focused on reducing plastic pollution, and has committed itself to using only reusable, recyclable or compostable plastic in its own brands by 2025. In 2019, it introduced recyclable paper bags as an alternative to traditional plastic 'bags for life'. It is also introducing plastic-free fruit and vegetable areas in a number of its stores to save 3 tonnes of plastic weekly!

In addition to its social responsibility objectives, Morrisons is aiming to improve its competitiveness, grow, improve customer choice and expand its range of 'local solutions' by increasing opportunities for local and regional events.

? Questions

1. Define the term 'market share'.
2. Explain the reasons why Morrisons may want to grow.
3. Morrisons is aiming to grow organically. Describe ways it may do this.
4. Explain three benefits of organic growth.
5. Identify four ways Morrisons is demonstrating its commitment to social responsibility.
6. Suggest reasons why Morrisons wants to be seen as socially responsible.

GO! Paired or group activity

Research an example of a business that has grown.

- Describe the method of growth used.
- What benefits does this have for the business?
- What implications does it have for the business?
- What criticism does the business receive in the media about this growth? Why?
- What could the business do to prevent media criticism?

Summarise your findings in a poster, short presentation or in a discussion forum. Be prepared to share these with the rest of your class.

Skills

- Applying
- Analysing & evaluating

? Questions

1. For each sector of the economy, describe objectives that businesses in that sector would have.
2. For each objective given in Q1, give a reason why this objective would be important.
3. Describe methods of growth that might be used by a multinational.
4. Describe two benefits of horizontal growth.
5. Describe two benefits of vertical growth.
6. Suggest a consequence of managerial objectives.
7. Suggest two reasons why customer satisfaction may be an objective.

External factors

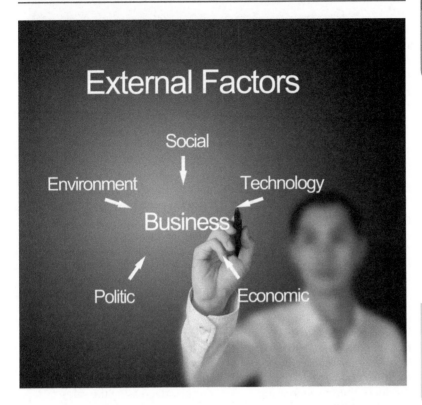

External factors are those outwith the organisation's control. Changes in the external environment impact on how the organisation functions both positively and negatively. The acronym PESTEC (political, economic, social, technological, environmental, competition) is a useful way of remembering the different types of external factors.

Political influences

Political influences come from the actions of government. We looked at the different levels of national and local government on page 19.

The government at each level has different powers that can influence how a business behaves.

Political influence	Positive impact	Negative impact
A change in, or introduction of, a new law	• The new law may reduce restrictions on trade (e.g. opening hours of a bar) and allow the business to gain greater sales and hopefully profit.	• Policies and procedures in the business may have to be changed; this could be costly in terms of money and time as staff may need to be retrained.
Funding to upgrade infrastructure (e.g. a new motorway or airport)	• This may reduce travelling time between destinations allowing products to be transported more quickly, which will satisfy customers. • Access to locations that were previously restricted may enable greater trade to take place and therefore the business will gain more customers.	• There may be significant disruption during the construction phase that may impact upon the business being able to transport goods to customers on time. • A business seen to support the building of a new motorway or airport may not be viewed favourably by stakeholders if it aims to be socially responsible; this may damage the image and reputation of the business.
A change in the amount of tax to be paid	• If income tax was to be reduced, consumers would have more disposable income that they could spend on products, thereby increasing the sales revenue of a business. • An increase in taxes may benefit public sector organisations by providing them with extra funding they can invest in improving facilities for communities.	• If income tax was to be increased, consumers would have less disposable income that they could spend on products, thereby decreasing the sales revenue of a business. • An increase in tax for any business will reduce the amount of profit it earns and may reduce the dividend payment to shareholders.
New government targets to protect the environment (e.g. to increase recycling by 10%)	• The business will be seen as being socially responsible and can use this as part of the marketing campaign to enhance image.	• Steps may need to be taken by the business to comply with government targets, e.g. to reduce wastage, and may cost money to implement.

Competition policy

The Government aims to prevent one company or a small number of companies from dominating a market. They do this through competition policy. Competition policy aims to reduce the power that one company or a small number of companies can have in a market. Competition in a market is seen as positive as it encourages companies to provide a better service to their customers and at a more competitive price. It also gives customers more choice in where they can buy goods and services from. Competition policy encourages businesses to be innovative and to invest in their workforce.

To prevent a company or a small number of companies dominating a market, the Government can prevent the merger of two companies to stop one larger company from being formed. For example, in 2019, Asda and Sainsbury's were prevented from merging. The Government was concerned that if they were allowed to merge, fuel prices would increase and a lower choice of products would be available to customers.

The Government can also prevent companies from:

- working with each other (known as a cartel) to prevent them fixing prices

- paying a low price to suppliers because they have power in a market.

Companies can be fined if they are in breach of competition policy and can be forced to change their prices.

Economic influences
Economic influences refers to anything that encourages people to spend or not to spend money.

Economic influence	Positive impact	Negative impact
The number of people who are unemployed	• If unemployment is high, a business will have a larger number of people they can recruit from to fill any job vacancies. • If unemployment is low, people may have more disposable income they can spend on products, resulting in greater demand for a product.	• If unemployment is low, it may be more difficult to recruit people with the correct skills for a job vacancy. • If unemployment is high, people may be more cautious when spending money and this could result in less demand for a product.
Change in the interest rate	• It is cheaper to borrow money when the interest rate is low and this may enable a business to borrow money to grow.	• If the interest rate is high, it is more expensive to borrow money. If the business is experiencing a cash flow problem and relies on loans, this could mean that suppliers do not get paid.
Changes to economic policies by government	• Changes to economic policy may increase consumer buying power, thereby increasing demand for a business.	• Changes to economic policy might restrict the ability of banks to lend money and this may cause a cash flow problem.

Make the link

Higher Economics explores economic policies in more depth.

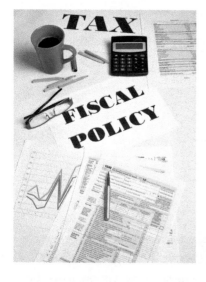

Group activity

Different economic policies exist. In groups, research one of the following economic policies and present your findings to your class:

- fiscal policy
- monetary policy
- supply-side policies

Try to find out the purpose of the policy and the different methods that the policy can employ to achieve different goals. Find examples of recent articles from the news that highlight the policy in action. Is the policy having a positive or negative impact? Why?

Skills

- Employability
- Applying
- Analysing & evaluating

Social influences

Social influences are those that are concerned with changing opinions, values and people's beliefs.

Social influence	Positive impact	Negative impact
Changes in fashion trends and tastes	• The business can take advantage of new opportunities by producing products that customers demand, thereby increasing sales.	• The business will need to invest money into carrying out market research to enable it to keep ahead of what people want; this will cost money and therefore reduce profits.
Changes in demographics (the number of people who live in a particular location)	• Customers who were previously unable to be accessed because of their location may now be easier to attract to the business, thereby increasing sales.	• It will be costly to set up new branches and offices in new locations, thereby reducing profit.
Increase in the number of family-friendly arrangements employers need to offer	• It is easier to recruit employees who have the appropriate skills but who want to work flexibly (e.g. part-time or job-share), thereby increasing the potential number of employees from which the business can choose.	• It may not suit the requirements of the business to have employees working flexibly and additional employees may need to be provided, which is costly.

Technological developments

Technology is changing how businesses operate, and is constantly changing. The table below provides some examples of how technology is having an impact on business.

Collaborative software	Sharing and editing documents using collaborative tools or apps. Documents and other files can be shared across the world and edited in real time by several people simultaneously.
5G networks	5G is the most recent mobile connectivity to rolled out across the UK beginning with several major cities in 2019. It provides faster connectivity and data transfer speeds.
Augmented reality (AR)	This technology provides interactive, reality-based displays that includes text, sounds and graphics. It gives the user the feeling they are in the actual location or environment, e.g. the cockpit of an aircraft.
3D printing	3D printing (or additive manufacturing) allows users to print a physical item, model or product from a three-dimensional image. The object is printed in layers.
Machine learning	The study of algorithms (rules) and statistical models that allows a computer to learn and perform tasks and follow instructions without being explicitly told what to do.
Two factor authentication	Using 2-factor authentication (2FA) requires the user to provide 2 methods of security authentication to verify themselves before they can access a system or application.

Businesses have to keep track and respond to technological innovations to remain competitive, even though this does cost time and money. Increasing use of digital technology requires businesses to constantly be responding to market trends and changes, and at the same time, ensure their staff are appropriately equipped to deal with these changes. There has never been a greater need for staff to keep up-to-date with changes in technology and upskill to keep ahead.

Individuals born after 1995 are known as Generation Z (or sometimes 'iGeneration'). This group of individuals account for a huge amount of spending in the economy and have grown up with technological innovation. For example, they:

> ● **Make the link**
>
> Generation Z and the gig economy have created new ways of working as well as ways for companies to attract new customers.

- Are familiar with constant application updates and can process information often faster than other generations. Consequentially, however, their attention spans can be shorter.

- Can use a variety of apps, often simultaneously, to multi-task.

- Often show entrepreneurial characteristics and traits at an early age and think of and develop business ideas quickly.

- Are more aware of global communication and interaction because of the opportunities the internet and social media has provided them.

Generation Z tends to consume products and services without necessarily owning them, i.e. access to online subscription services (e.g. television and music). Generation Z has made way for the 'gig economy', a new type of independent workforce, through the growth of services such as Uber, Airbnb and Deliveroo. It is known as the 'gig economy' because each piece of work is allocated to a specific individual (e.g. a specific order from a fast food company to the specific individual who will deliver it).

Make the link

There are examples throughout these Course Notes of how technology can be used in business.

GO! Individual activity

Choose three examples of recent technological innovations. Find out how each of these is having an impact on business.

Do some research to find out how businesses have responded to changes in demographics over the last 20 years (e.g. from millennials to Generation Z).

Find examples of the gig economy operating in your area. How has the gig economy changed the way businesses work in your area and how consumers access products and services?

Skills

- Employability
- Applying
- Analysing & evaluating

Environmental influences

Businesses are becoming more aware of the need to be environmentally friendly and sustainable (in response to having to be more socially responsible) and are operating increasingly ethically.

 Make the link

Environmental issues in relation to operations are explored in Chapter 4.

Environmental influence	Positive impact	Negative impact
Changes in the weather	• Depending on the product being sold, a certain temperature may increase demand (e.g. demand for ice cream goes up when it is hot), thereby increasing sales.	• Depending on the product being sold, a certain temperature may reduce the quantity of a product that can be supplied (e.g. a very wet summer would reduce the quantity of strawberries available to be sold), thereby reducing sales. • Bad weather might mean that orders cannot be delivered on time, resulting in unhappy customers.
Increased pressure to recycle	• The business will be seen as being socially responsible and can use this as part of the marketing campaign to enhance their image.	• It will cost money to provide recycling facilities, thereby reducing profit.

Competition influences

A competitor is a business that provides the same product as another business.

Competition influence	Positive impact	Negative impact
New competitor entering the market	• This might be good for consumers because competition can encourage businesses to provide loyalty schemes and reduce prices.	• A business may have to provide discounts to customers to retain their loyalty and this can be costly.
Competitor introducing a new product	• This will give customers a wide range of products to choose from. • It might give a business an idea that they can develop themselves even better to gain customers.	• It will cost money to carry out market research to try and stay ahead of what competitors are doing and it might not always be successful.

Make the link

External influences can have a positive and negative impact on customers as well as on businesses.

GO! **Paired or group activity**

Do some research and find an example of an external influence that has had an impact on a business recently. Present your findings to your class or ask your Teacher/Lecturer to create a discussion forum to post your findings.

Make sure you:

- Clearly describe the external influence.
- Discuss the positive impact the external influence has had.
- Discuss the negative impact the external influence has had.

Skills

- Applying
- Analysing & evaluating

? **Questions**

1. What are external factors?
2. Give two examples of each external factor.
3. Describe the impact of economic policy on a business.
4. Discuss the impact of environmental influences on a business.
5. Suggest reasons why businesses have to take account of external factors.
6. Describe each of the following technologies:
   - 5G
   - Machine learning
   - Augmented reality
   - 2FA
7. Suggest actions that a business will have to take in each of the following situations to remain competitive:
   - Increase in interest rates
   - Changes in fashion
   - Changes in demographics
8. Give examples of how Generation Z may impact on business.

Internal factors

Internal factors are things within the business that impact upon how it operates.

- **Financial** – there might not be enough finance to make new purchases. This might mean that raw materials cannot be purchased and production stops. If production stops, orders might be delayed and customers become unhappy. A lack of finance might also mean that objectives, e.g. growth, cannot be met.

- **Employees** – employees might not have the correct skills or motivation required to carry out a task. If they don't have the correct skills, the quality of their work might be poor, which results in a product of poor quality. Customers are likely to be put off if a product is of poor quality. If the motivation of employees is low (ie they don't want to work as hard as they could), their productivity will be low and deadlines might be missed. Low motivation could also result in a higher absence rate.

Internal Factors

- **Management** – managers might not have enough experience or skill in decision-making. This could result in poor decisions being made that impact upon the whole organisation, e.g. fewer sales.

- **Existing technology** – the technology that a business has might not be the best available or suitable to carry out certain tasks. If technology is out of date, the production process might not be as effective as it could be and machinery could break down. If machinery breaks down, production will stop. A lack of technology might also mean that a business cannot keep up with what their competitors are doing, e.g. if they are unable to use social media to sell products but their competitors are, then they might lose customers. Selling products via social media is known as social commerce or s-commerce.

Other internal factors that impact on the business include the culture within the organisation and also the decision-making process. These, therefore, need to be explored further.

Corporate culture

This can be defined as *'the values, beliefs and norms related to the organisation that is shared by all its members'.*

Corporate culture is sometimes referred to as organisational culture. It consists of everything to do with the organisation including its values, emotions, beliefs and the language used. It is also to do with the attitude and behaviours that members of the organisation adopt because of the culture within the organisation. It is established from the beginning of the organisation's life and reflects the different activities (formal and informal), policies and procedures that the organisation has. The different management styles adopted by senior managers may also influence the culture of an organisation.

The benefits of having a strong corporate culture are:

- Employees feel they are part of, and belong to, the organisation; this can provide them with a sense of security and can improve motivation.

- It can motivate staff, which in turn will lead to improved efficiency and higher productivity.

- It can create positive relationships within the organisation that will enable better communication and decision-making.

- Employee loyalty can be increased, which will decrease staff turnover and staff absence rates.

- The image and identity of the organisation can be improved, which will be visible to all stakeholders.

- Customer loyalty might be higher because they associate themselves with the identity (e.g. logos, uniform and store design) of the organisation. It may also be recognisable across the globe if it is a multinational organisation.

- There will be consistency across the organisation, which will allow employees to work in different locations or branches if necessary.

When corporate culture in an organisation is poor, it can have costs for the organisation:

- Employee motivation can be low, which results in lower productivity and poorer quality goods and services being provided.

- Employee turnover can be high, which results in higher recruitment and selection costs.

- Communication within the organisation can be poor and therefore decisions might be more difficult to make.

- Working relationships between employees can become hostile and impact on the atmosphere in the organisation.

- Change can be difficult to implement and the organisation therefore might not be able to keep up to date with competitors.

When trying to establish a positive corporate culture within an organisation, several factors need to be considered:

- The vision and aims of the organisation; these normally come from the original owners and/or shareholders.

- The opinions and views of employees; consulting employees on matters will help to encourage good working relationships and improve motivation.

- The design of stores, logos and uniforms. This is because these are visible and promote the identity of the organisation, though can be expensive to design and then to implement.

- How people (e.g. employees and other stakeholders) are made aware of the culture. This might involve holding events, which could be costly.

- The policies and procedures that the organisation has. These lay down the expectation and behaviour expected and will have an impact on corporate culture.

? Questions

1. Describe three internal factors that can impact an organisation.
2. Define the term 'corporate culture'.
3. Explain three benefits of having a corporate culture.
4. Describe factors that need to be considered when establishing a corporate culture.

Stakeholders

At National 5, we explored stakeholder interest and influence. At Higher level we need to think about the **interdependence** each stakeholder has and also the **conflict** that can exist between different stakeholders.

- **Interdependence** – why a stakeholder needs another stakeholder.

- **Conflict** – the disagreements that can occur between different stakeholders.

In the table below, owners could be shareholders and/or managers depending on the type of business being discussed.

<table>
<tr><td colspan="3">

⚠ Watch point

Competitors are not accepted as an example of a stakeholder in exams. This is because stakeholders are not interested in the success of a business.

</td></tr>
</table>

Stakeholders	Interdependence	Conflict
Owners and employees	• Owners need employees to carry out different tasks **and** employees need owners to pay their wages. • Owners need employees to be as productive as they can **and** employees need owners to provide the necessary job training.	• Owners want to pay as low a wage as possible so that their profit is high **whereas** employees want high wages for their work. • Owners want employees to work as many hours as they can **whereas** employees want to work as few hours as possible.
Owners and customers	• Owners need customers to buy products from them to make profit **and** customers need owners to provide them with the product they want. • Owners need customers to become loyal to increase market share **and** customers want to be rewarded for loyalty (e.g. discounts).	• Owners want to make as much profit as possible by charging the highest price they can **whereas** customers want as low a price as possible. • Owners want to keep costs low by providing the cheapest possible service they can **whereas** customers want the best possible service (e.g. after-sales).
Employees and customers	• Employees need customers to buy from an organisation so that they get paid **and** customers need employees to provide them with good customer service.	• Employees want customers to spend as much as possible to increase their commission **whereas** customers want as much discount as possible.
Owners and suppliers	• Owners need suppliers to provide products on time **and** suppliers need owners to provide them with repeat orders. • Owners need suppliers to provide a quality product at a suitable price to make a profit **and** suppliers need owners to pay their invoices within an agreed time to prevent cash flow problems.	• Owners want supplies for as low a price as possible **whereas** suppliers want to maximise their profits. • Owners want to wait for as long as possible before paying their debts **whereas** suppliers want paid as quickly as possible.

(continued)

Owners and banks	• Owners need banks to provide them with affordable loans **and** banks need owners who can make repayments on time.	• Owners want interest rates on loans to be as low as possible **whereas** banks want to make as much profit as possible by charging higher interest rates.
Owners and government	• Owners need the Government to have low tax rates **and** the Government needs owners to provide jobs. • Owners need the Government to provide grants **and** the Government needs owners to regenerate local communities and unused pieces of land.	• Owners want low tax rates to maximise profits **whereas** the Government wants taxes to invest into the country, e.g. for the NHS. • Owners want to dominate the market **whereas** the Government wants competition to encourage lower prices for customers.
Owners and the local community	• Owners need local communities to support their business **and** the local community needs owners to provide jobs to decrease unemployment.	• Owners want to keep costs low to maximise profit **whereas** local communities want businesses to invest in community projects.

GO! Group activity

You have 10 minutes to think of as many examples as possible of:

- interdependence between stakeholders
- conflict that might exist between stakeholders.

Other stakeholders you might want to think about include pressure groups, trade unions and the media.

Skills

- Applying
- Analysing & evaluating

⚠ Watch point

You must give both stakeholders in your answer when talking about interdependence or conflict.

🔍 Case study

Premier Inn

Premier Inn, a brand of Whitbread, has over 800 hotels offering accommodation for its customers at a reasonable price. It currently offers over 77,000 rooms in a variety of locations (city centres, airports and suburban) across the UK as well as the Middle East and Germany, and aims to expand this to over 85,000 rooms by 2020. It has also developed a new style of room – hub by Premier Inn – in London and Edinburgh that offers smaller, compact rooms with a range of features e.g. 40-inch smart TVs, monsoon showers and mood lighting.

Premier Inn has a commitment to people and the planet through its 'Force for Good' programme. The programme is based upon three concepts:

- Opportunity – everyone is welcome regardless of where they are from.

- Community – contributing to communities and customers being served.

- Responsibility – behaving responsibility towards people and the planet.

It provides opportunities to a range of people regardless of who they are or where they are from by employing them in their hotels, coffee shops and restaurants. It invests in skills to give its employees the best chance 'to shine'. It serves its communities by undertaking charity fundraising and assisting its customers to make healthy choices on a range of food and drink. It aims to act responsibly by sourcing quality, good-value products from suppliers who also have the same values and standards. Both beef and milk used by Premier Inn is sourced from the UK and Ireland. It is committed to sustainability by increasing the number of locations with solar panels, diverting 100% of waste from landfill sites and cutting carbon emissions in half.

❓ Questions

1. Describe two external influences being discussed in the case study.
2. For each external influence provided in question 1, give two examples of how Premier Inn has reacted to each influence.
3. From the case study, describe two examples of an interdependent stakeholder relationship.
4. From the case study, describe two possible examples of a conflict between stakeholders.
5. From the case study, identify ways Premier Inn is demonstrating corporate social responsibility.
6. Describe and justify the method of growth being adopted by Premier Inn.

(The information for this case study was taken from https://www.premierinn.com/gb/en/why/force-for-good.html and https://www.whitbread.co.uk/our-brands/premier-inn)

Structures

An organisation consists of a group of people who come together for a common goal or aim. They organise themselves internally to suit the type of activities that the organisation is carrying out.

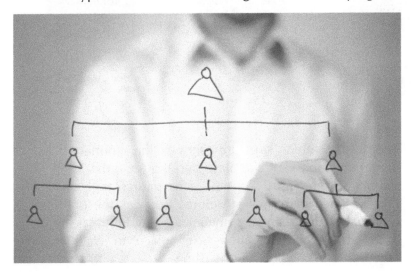

Organisations can group themselves in a number of different ways. This depends on several factors:

- Size of the organisation (larger organisations tend to require a more formal structure compared to smaller ones).

- The technology being used (this could be used to communicate with other parts of the organisation in other locations).

- Who the customer is (in other words, the target market).

- The good or service that is being provided.

- The amount of finance available to the organisation (this might limit the type of structure or grouping that could be used).

An organisation chart shows how an organisation is structured. It shows:

- Who has overall **responsibility** for the organisation.

- The different levels of **authority** and **responsibility** within the organisation.

- The lines of **communication** and the **chain of command**.

- The **span of control** for different managers.

- Different **relationships** that exist within the organisation.

- Where work could be **delegated** to **subordinates**.

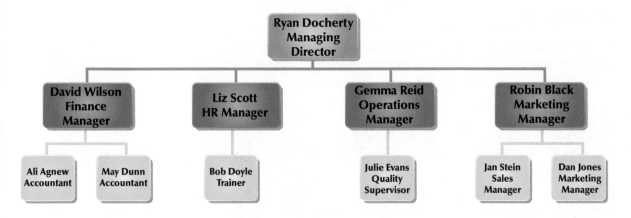

The organisation structure shows the formal lines of communication that take place and the route that is taken for information and instructions to reach a particular place. Despite the existence of **formal structures** (such as the one above), **informal structures** can sometimes exist. Informal structures exist when communication takes place in ways that the organisation structure does not show.

There are a number of key terms that you need to learn about when you are analysing how organisations are structured.

- **Responsibility** – being answerable for decisions and actions taken within the organisation.

- **Authority** – having power to make decisions.

- **Chain of command** – this shows how instructions are passed down through an organisation and how communication can flow up and down the organisation. A long chain of command may mean that communication and decision-making is slower compared to a short chain of command. Decisions might therefore be slower to implement.

- **Delegation** – giving the authority and responsibility to someone else to carry out a particular task (e.g. a manager giving the authority and responsibility to a subordinate to carry out a task).

Grouping of activities

Organisations can group their staff activities in a number of different ways. The factors that influence the type of grouping to be chosen are given on page 47.

Functional grouping

Functional grouping means grouping by department, and people working in these departments have a similar area of interest. These functions might include: Human Resources (HR), Operations, Marketing, Finance and Research & Development. People can contact specific departments if they require specialist advice or help (e.g. Marketing might contact HR when recruiting a new employee for that department). Clear lines of authority exist (as shown on the organisation chart) between subordinates and managers, and everyone will usually have clearly defined tasks and duties to carry out. Sometimes departmental aims might overtake the aims of the organisation and because of this, the organisation can sometimes find it difficult to respond to changing market conditions and external factors.

Product grouping

This type of grouping exists when the organisation is structured around the products that it sells. Each department in the organisation concentrates on one specific product, which results in specialist knowledge of each product within that department. Each department is also able to respond quickly to changes in the market, but if their product is not performing well, this is easily identifiable to managers. If the organisation introduces a new product, new employees need to be employed. There may also be rivalry between different departments that can be counterproductive to working relationships within the organisation. Line relationships (who an employee reports to) in product groupings may not be as clear as more traditional, functional structures.

This is an example of a product grouping:

Customer grouping

This is grouping by customer types (in other words, grouping by market segment or target market). Products can be marketed towards each specific customer group. The organisation can build up loyalty with their customers because activities are focused on the specific customer group, and therefore a higher level of customer service is achieved. High staffing costs can be a disadvantage of this type of structure.

The following structure shows a customer grouping for a holiday company:

⚠ Watch point

Make sure you can describe different types of staff groupings as well as give reasons for why they would be used.

Place/territory grouping

This type of grouping exists when the organisation is structured around specific locations. The needs of customers within each specific location can be focused on and the organisation can become familiar with different cultures that exist in different locations. Technology can be used to communicate with staff in different locations (e.g. videoconferencing), though this can be expensive. Duplication of resources can be a downside to this structure.

The following structure shows a place/territory grouping for a UK-based company:

GO! Individual activity

Create a mindmap with the different types of staff groupings. Give a description of each and include some benefits and costs. Make your mindmap more attractive by including relevant diagrams. You can use appropriate software packages to help if you prefer.
Keep a copy of your mindmap as a revision tool.

Skills

- Applying
- Analysing & evaluating

? Questions

1. Describe the influences on the choice of its structure that an organisation may have.
2. Describe the content of an organisation chart.
3. Define the following terms:

   - Delegation
   - Chain of command
   - Authority
   - Responsibility

4. Name different functional areas that might exist within an organisation.
5. Compare two methods of staff groupings.
6. Suggest two benefits of a place/territory structure.
7. Suggest two benefits of a functional structure.
8. Justify the use of a customer grouping.
9. Explain the benefits of product grouping.
10. Distinguish between a product and customer grouping.

Span of control

This is the number of subordinates (people) who report to one person. For example, a manager might have five people who report to them so they therefore have five subordinates.

A wide span of control will mean that many people report to one person whereas a narrow span of control will mean that very few people report to one person.

Wide span of control

- More empowerment is possible due to the number of subordinates.

- Tasks can be delegated more easily to the subordinate most suitably skilled to carry these out; however, employees may feel reluctant and uncomfortable with this.

- As there are a large number of subordinates, this can cause extra stress for the manager who may have little time to deal with staff-related issues.

- Managers may feel that, as they have more subordinates to manage, they are more powerful and this can be motivating to them.

- The organisation will have fewer managers and therefore saves money.

- A shorter chain of command will exist and therefore communication and decision-making is likely to be more effective.

Narrow span of control

- Less empowerment as there are fewer subordinates to manage and the manager is unlikely to delegate as much.

- Delegation may be more difficult as there are fewer subordinates.

- Subordinates have more opportunities to communicate and interact with their manager.

- Subordinates are more likely to have the chance to participate in decision-making and planning.

- A long chain of command will exist and therefore communication and decision-making might be slower.

Organisation structures

Tall and flat structures

A **tall**, or hierarchical, structure has many layers of management. This means that it has a long chain of command; it will take time for instructions and information to pass through the structure. These structures are often found in public sector organisations but, as a consequence of the global economic downturn in the early 2000s, many public sector organisations have restructured to save staffing costs. (Changing structure is covered on pages 56–57.)

Flat structures contain fewer layers of management compared to tall ones. This means that flat structures have a shorter chain of command; it will take less time for instructions and information to pass through the structure. This type of structure is often found in smaller organisations. Because there are fewer layers of management compared to tall structures, the cost of management salaries will be less.

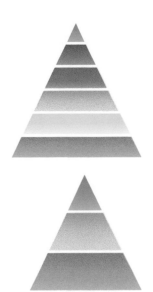

Matrix structures

Matrix (or project-based) structures tend to be formed when a specific task or project is to be carried out. People from across the organisation will come together from various departments to form the matrix structure. When the task or project has been completed, the matrix structure will become obsolete. A project or team leader will be appointed to provide leadership to the task or project being undertaken. Because people from across the organisation may participate in this structure, it can be motivating for employees and useful to the organisation when problems are

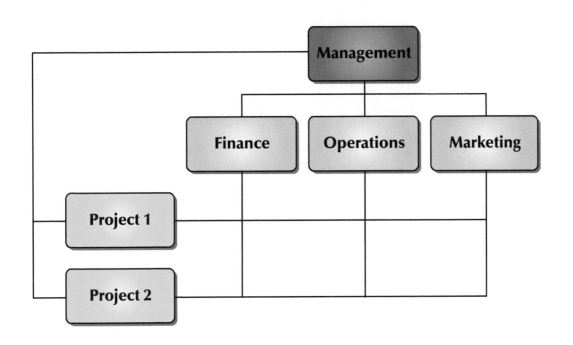

being solved. Even though it gives employees the opportunity to learn new skills, by participating in a project or task, it can be costly to implement and for the organisation to coordinate. Employees may find having two managers (e.g. from their own functional area as well as for the matrix structure) confusing.

Entrepreneurial structures

An **entrepreneurial structure** is often found in smaller organisations. This type of structure is seen when decisions are made by the owner or certain managers with very little input (if anything) from employees. Even though it means decisions can be made quickly, because employees are not involved in the process, it can reduce employees' motivation. It also means that good ideas or creative solutions to problems are not considered because employees have not been consulted. This type of structure is not often found in larger organisations because it would place too much of a heavy workload on managers who have to make decisions.

Centralisation and decentralisation

In a **centralised structure**, decisions are made by the senior management of the organisation. This structure is often associated with tall (hierarchical) structures. In a plc, for example, decisions might be made by managers at the head office rather than managers in different branches. Employees at various levels of the hierarchy are not consulted about decisions being made, which can result in them becoming demotivated.

In a **decentralised structure**, decision-making is delegated to departments and subordinates. This type of structure is associated with a flat structure and because people at different levels of the hierarchy are involved in decision-making, it can motivate them. Because decisions are made by different departments, it can be harder to ensure consistency across the organisation (e.g. departments might make decisions to suit their own needs rather than those of the whole organisation) whereas a centralised structure would achieve this consistency.

⚠ Watch point

Exam questions can ask you about centralised and decentralised structures, as well as centralised and decentralised decision making.

Relationships within organisations

Different types of relationships exist between people in organisations.

Line Relationships	This is a relationship between a subordinate and their line manager, *e.g. Ryan Docherty and David Wilson on the chart shown on page 48.*
Lateral Relationships	This is a relationship between two or more people on the same level of the organisation, *e.g. Liz Scott and Gemma Reid on the chart shown on page 48.*
Functional Relationships	This is a relationship between two functional areas in an organisation, e.g. one providing support to another. *An example is Human Resources providing advice to the Marketing department when recruiting a new member of staff.*
Staff Relationships	This is a relationship between two or more people in an organisation who provide advice or support to others.
Informal Relationships	An informal relationship exists when two or more people communicate on an informal basis, normally outwith the organisation, *e.g. two people meeting for coffee after work.* This is in comparison to a formal relationship, such as those described above.

❓Questions

1. Compare a wide and narrow span of control.
2. What implications might a wide span of control have for an organisation?
3. Discuss the impact that a narrow span of control might have on decision-making.
4. Compare a tall and a flat structure.
5. Describe five characteristics of a matrix structure.
6. Suggest benefits and costs of an entrepreneurial structure.
7. Compare a centralised and decentralised structure.
8. Discuss the benefits and costs of centralised and decentralised structures.
9. Describe types of relationships that can exist in an organisation.
10. Compare a formal and informal relationship.

Changing structure

An organisation might decide to change its structure. It may do this because:

- The size of the organisation has changed.

- The availability of finance has changed.

- Market conditions have changed.

- New technology has become available.

The managers of an organisation may decide to change its structure to ensure that it continues to meet the aims and objectives it has set itself.

An organisation may decide to change its structure by **delayering** or **downsizing**.

Delayering

Delayering means removing layers of management from the structure. For example, moving from a tall structure to a flat structure. As well as saving money on management salaries, it allows for quicker communication and decision-making because there are fewer layers. Market conditions may be responded to more quickly compared to in a taller structure. Employees may feel more empowered to make decisions and to use their own initiative; this can increase motivation and productivity. This is because managers will have a wider span of control and ultimately might mean that the supervision and management of employees could be more difficult. Delayering also means that there will be fewer promotion opportunities for existing staff.

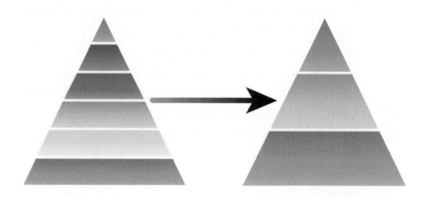

Downsizing

Downsizing involves removing some of the activities that the organisation carries out from its structure. For example, closing a branch, factory or division in response to external factors.

Some activities might be **outsourced** to enable the organisation to concentrate on its core activities. The organisation carrying out the activity on behalf of the organisation that is downsizing will be paid for doing this, which could be expensive. It also means that the organisation needs to trust the outsourced organisation to deliver on time and to the standard expected. Effective communication between the two organisations is crucial to the success of outsourcing.

? Questions

1. Suggest reasons why an organisation may wish to change structure.
2. Compare delayering and downsizing.
3. Justify the use of delayering.
4. Discuss the impact of delayering on existing staff.
5. Suggest reasons why an organisation may outsource.

Decision-making

Managers and decision-making

Managers have the authority to make decisions on behalf of an organisation to enable it to meet its objectives. Decision-making involves choosing the best option from a range of options.

The role of a manager in decision-making involves them carrying out a number of tasks:

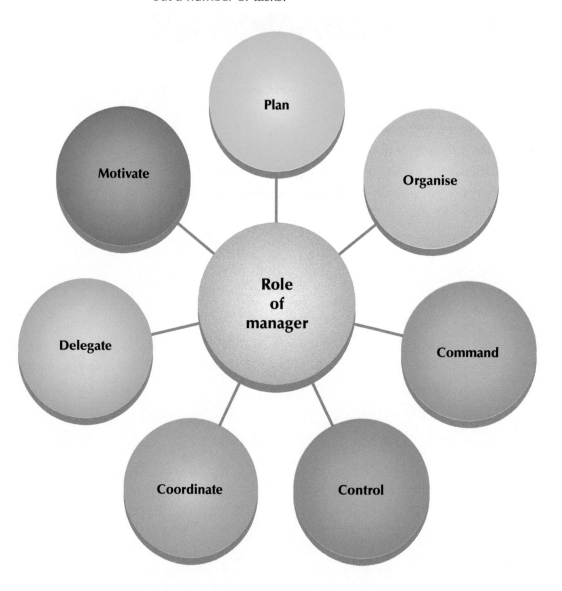

Role	What does it mean?
Plan	Thinking about the future by setting the organisation's objectives and deciding what needs to be done to achieve each objective.
Organise	Ensuring resources (e.g. human and financial) are available to allow objectives to be achieved.
Command	Instructing employees to carry out specific tasks so that they know what is expected to achieve objectives.
Control	Checking and monitoring work and tasks that have been completed to ensure they meet the standard required to achieve objectives. Where necessary, action can be taken to ensure activities are on track to help achieve each objective.
Coordinate	Ensuring resources (e.g. employees) are in place at the right time and working towards the same objective. This will ensure objectives are achieved as efficiently as they can.
Delegate	The responsibility for carrying out a task can be given to someone else (delegated), so that the manager can concentrate on other activities.
Motivate	Encouraging and inspiring employees to work as hard as they can so that as many objectives are achieved as possible and to the highest standard.

Managers have a very important role to perform in an organisation and have been selected based on the skills, qualities and experience that they have. Managers need to be able to work with a range of people as well as being able to make decisions.

Types of decisions

	Strategic	Tactical	Operational
What is it?	Long-term decisions concerned with the overall direction and focus of the organisation. Strategic decisions determine the objectives of the organisation.	Medium-term decisions concerned with actions to achieve strategic decisions.	Short-term decisions that affect the day-to-day running of the organisation.
Who makes it?	Senior management	Senior and middle management	First line management, e.g. team leaders, supervisors

(continued)

Examples?	• To expand into a new country • To diversify the product range • To merge with another company • To introduce a new management information system • To change organisation structure	• To find cheaper suppliers to cut costs • To expand the range of goods offered – to grow • To develop a new marketing campaign to increase the number of customers	• What hours staff will work next week • To give someone a day off
Risk	High risk	Medium risk	Low risk

Decision-making can take place centrally (i.e. in a centralised structure) or can be delegated to departments (i.e. in a decentralised structure). Make sure you go back and look at this section carefully on page 54.

SWOT analysis

An organisation might carry out a SWOT analysis (strengths, weaknesses, opportunities and threats) as part of the decision-making process. It can be used to identify the different internal and external factors that may impact upon the decision-making process.

Strengths and weaknesses are about the organisation and its current position, whereas opportunities and threats are concerned with the external environment. An organisation will want to build on its strengths, improve its weaknesses, take advantage of opportunities and minimise the impact of threats.

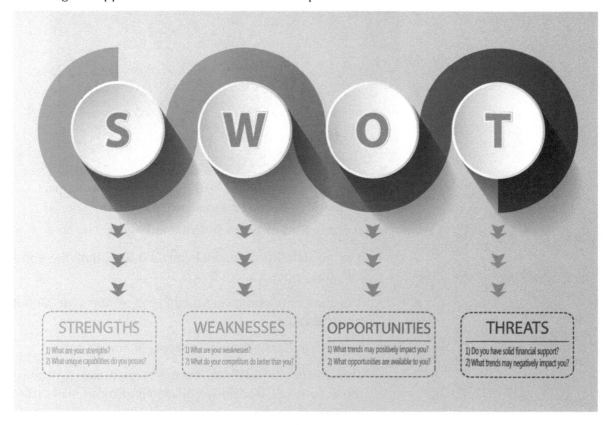

STRENGTHS
1) What are your strengths?
2) What unique capabilities do you posses?

WEAKNESSES
1) What are your weaknesses?
2) What do your competitors do better than you?

OPPORTUNITIES
1) What trends may positively impact you?
2) What opportunities are available to you?

THREATS
1) Do you have solid financial support?
2) What trends may negatively impact you?

GO! Group activity

Carry out a SWOT analysis on an organisation you are familiar with. This could be a local business or even your school.

Then think about how your organisation could:

- build on its strengths
- reduce its weaknesses
- expand on its opportunities
- reduce or avoid its threats.

Skills

- Applying
- Analysing & evaluating

Constraints on decision-making

A number of internal and external factors can impact on decision-making. External factors are explored on page 33.

Internal constraints might include the following:

- The availability of finance might mean that the most effective option cannot be chosen.

- The number of employees might limit what can or cannot be achieved.

- The skill and training requirements of employees.

- The ability and skill of managers to make decisions; more complex decisions will demand more skills from managers.

- The policies and procedures of the organisation might limit what decision can be made and, as a result, the decision might have to be modified to comply with them.

- The quality of information available; a lack of quality information might mean that a fully informed decision cannot be made.

- Employees might be resistant to change, which will make implementing the decision more difficult and time-consuming, especially if they disagree with the option chosen.

- Appropriate technology might not be available to implement the best decision and therefore money needs to be spent upgrading technology.

- Whether or not decision-making models (e.g. SWOT analysis) were used in the way that they are intended. Missing out a key step could make the process flawed.

Measuring the success of decisions

Once a decision has been made, the quality of the decision needs to be evaluated. This means looking carefully at the decision made and thinking about whether it achieved what it set out to achieve and how well it achieved it.

Decisions can be evaluated by:

- Asking employees (e.g. through surveys and staff meetings) for their views (in other words, obtaining qualitative information) on how well the decision has worked and how effective they think it is.

- Looking at quantitative information (e.g. productivity rates and sales or profit figures) to see if the decision has impacted negatively or positively.

- Looking at employee absence rates (again, quantitative information) to see if there has been an increase or decrease in the number of days employees take off work.

- Measuring the level of employee motivation within the workplace to see whether or not the decision has reduced or increased this.

- Asking customers for their opinion by carrying out research (e.g. conducting a survey) as this will give first-hand information from their opinion.

- Examining the number of complaints received.

- Reviewing online customer reviews, e.g. on social media, as well as in the press for feedback.

> **⚠ Watch point**
>
> The method used to evaluate a decision will depend on what decision was made and on whom it impacts.

❔ Questions

1. Describe the role of a manager in decision-making.
2. Describe three types of decision.
3. Give an example of each type of decision.
4. Describe the components of a SWOT analysis.
5. Describe ways of measuring the success of a decision.
6. Explain internal constraints that impact upon decision-making.

★ **Key questions**

1. Compare the features of large organisations from different sectors of the economy.
2. Describe and justify objectives that large organisations from different sectors of the economy may have.
3. Describe and justify the internal structures that large organisations may have.
4. Explain the impact that internal factors can have on a large organisation.
5. Explain the impact that external factors can have on a large organisation.
6. Describe the conflicts of interest that may exist between different stakeholders.

Summary

This chapter provided you with an overview of the role of business in society and the types of large organisations that exist within it. It considered the different types of objectives large organisations can have and why they are important. Different ways organisations can grow were examined, as well as the external and internal factors that can impact upon how large organisations operate. The different stakeholders that depend on the organisation were outlined as well as the conflict that each stakeholder can have with each other. The way organisations can be structured was examined. Finally, the importance of decision-making in organisations and how organisations make decisions was explored.

The main topics in this chapter were:

- The role of business in society
- Types of business organisations
- Objectives
- Methods of growth
- External factors
- Internal factors
- Stakeholders
- Structures
- Decision-making

By successfully answering the key questions, you will show that you have grasped the main topics covered in this chapter.

2 END OF CHAPTER MATERIAL

Sample exam question

Make sure you read each exam question carefully as every word is there for a reason. It is good practice to break each question down into parts before you answer it so that you know what is required.

> ⚠ **Watch point**
>
> You must write your answer according to the command word(s) used in the question.

For example:

- **Describe and justify two objectives for a public limited company. (4 marks)**

The command words – the instructions to you on how to answer the question.	The number of objectives required.	The type of company that your objectives must be relevant for.

Sample answer

A plc might have an objective to grow (**0 marks – the objective is only identified**). This means it wants to get bigger by, for example, opening more stores (**1 description mark**). It would want to grow to gain more customers and to increase its market share (**1 justification mark**).

> ⚠ **Watch point**
>
> When being asked to 'describe', you do not get any marks for simply identifying (naming or stating) something.

The plc might also have the objective to be socially responsible (**0 marks – the objective is only identified**). This means to behave responsibly towards the environment and not to do anything that may harm it (**1 description mark**). It might have this objective to gain a good reputation and to improve the image of the company (**1 justification mark**).

Examiner's comments

The candidate has given a description of two different objectives that are suitable for a plc (a large organisation). They have then given at least one reason why each objective is appropriate and suitable for a plc. (**4/4 marks**)

More sample exam questions

- Describe different methods of staff grouping. (5 marks)
- Explain the impact a narrow span of control might have for a manager. (5 marks)
- Suggest benefits of being socially responsible. (3 marks)
- Describe ways an organisation can demonstrate corporate social responsibility. (5 marks)
- Describe and justify methods of growth for a multinational. (6 marks)
- Compare a tall and flat structure. (3 marks)
- Discuss the impact political factors may have on an organisation. (4 marks)
- Describe internal factors that can impact upon an organisation. (3 marks)
- Explain the role of a manger on decision-making. (5 marks)
- Distinguish between two types of decisions. (4 marks)
- Explain internal constraints that can make decision-making difficult. (5 marks)
- Describe ways of measuring the success of decision. (4 marks)
- Describe the conflict of interest that can exist between different stakeholders. (6 marks)
- Describe the interdependence that can exist between different stakeholders. (4 marks)

Check your progress

	NEED HELP	GETTING THERE	CONFIDENT
Sectors of industry	◯	◯	◯
Sectors of the economy	◯	◯	◯
Private sector organisations	◯	◯	◯
Public sector organisations	◯	◯	◯
Third sector organisations	◯	◯	◯
Objectives	◯	◯	◯
Methods of growth	◯	◯	◯
External factors	◯	◯	◯
Internal factors	◯	◯	◯
Stakeholders	◯	◯	◯
Structures	◯	◯	◯
Decision-making	◯	◯	◯

3 Management of Marketing

From National 5 you should already be able to:

- Describe types and methods of market research and outline their costs and benefits.
- Outline the stages of the product life cycle.
- Describe elements of the marketing mix.
- Outline ways ICT can be used to contribute to effective marketing.

What you will learn about in this chapter:

- Customers.
- Market research.
- The extended marketing mix.
- Technology in marketing.

What is marketing?

Marketing is more than just advertising or selling a product in a shop. It is about linking what to produce to what is consumed to make sure the needs and wants of the customer are met.

Most organisations will have a marketing department that carries out a range of activities. The purpose of the marketing department is to:

- help achieve the organisation's objectives
- raise awareness of products
- increase the number of customers in a market (i.e. achieve market growth)
- inform customers about products
- anticipate what customers want.

Marketing **identifies** what customers want, **anticipates** the requirements of the customer and then attempts to **satisfy** these.

Marketing is a strategic activity because it impacts upon the whole organisation and its vision.

⚠ Watch point

Look out for examples of how technology can be used in marketing throughout this chapter.

☄ Make the link

The aims of an organisation will be closely linked with its marketing activities.

Customers

Customers are very important to all businesses. In National 5, we explored different types of customers by looking at market segmentation. We also looked at the importance of good customer service.

Organisations may market their products towards a particular target market (**differentiated marketing**) or at more than one target market (**undifferentiated marketing**). Focusing marketing activities on particular market segments can have its benefits.

- Products can be specifically tailored to the requirements of the customer.
- Prices can be set to reflect the market segment.
- Promotions can be tailored towards the market segment.
- The most appropriate place to sell the product can be chosen.

⚠ Watch point

Different businesses will focus on different market segments.

Market-led and product-led

A business can be market-led or product-led in its approach to marketing. In other words, it might have a market orientation or product orientation.

Market-led (market orientated)	Product-led (product orientated)
• Product produced based on what the customer wants. • Customer wants and needs are identified through market research. • Changes in social factors (e.g. trends and fashion) can be identified and acted upon more easily. • The market may have significant competition.	• Product produced because the organisation thinks they are good at providing it. • Little or no market research carried out as the needs and wants of the customer are not of importance. • The market may have little or no competition.

Consumer behaviour

Businesses will be interested in the behaviour of consumers to help them make decisions about their product and how it is marketed. Studying consumer behaviour allows them to attempt to answer several questions.

Question	Comments
Why do they buy what they do?	Some products might be bought for status, e.g. designer clothing might be bought as a result of peer pressure or as a status symbol.
What motivates them to buy?	What factors trigger people to want to buy something? Is the purchase necessary or is another factor responsible for making someone want to buy?
What influences buying decisions?	What pressures or stimuli influence where, when and how people buy? Has advertising had an influence, or a point-of-sale display? Does the store layout have an impact? Does culture have an influence?
What customer buys the product?	Which market segment does the product appeal to?
Where do they choose to buy? Why?	Where do they choose to buy the product? Is it online or in a shop? Why? What factors have resulted in this choice, e.g. convenience?
What do they look for when buying?	What criteria have to be satisfied when buying something? What questions have been asked?

Consumer behaviour is about trying to answer the 'why', 'what', 'how' and 'where' questions. It is important to be able to answer these to develop a successful marketing strategy.

Consumers have different types of buying behaviour depending on what they are buying.

Impulse purchases	Buying something without thinking, often in the spur of the moment. It might be because something has influenced the customer to buy (e.g. a promotion).
Routine and habitual purchases	Buying something because it is habit, e.g. going to buy a loaf of bread. These types of purchases will happen without much thought.
Limited decision-making purchases	Buying something that requires some thought before a decision is made. For example, thinking about whether or not a piece of clothing is appropriate for a certain purpose.
Informed purchases	Buying something that requires a high degree of thought before a decision is made. For example, buying a new car or a house. These types of purchases might not be made very often.

Electronic point of sale systems (EPOS) can gather information about consumer behaviour that the organisation can attempt to analyse and then understand. When people make purchases in a supermarket or shop, the EPOS system is collecting data about them and their buying habits. Promotions, offers and mail shots can then be designed specifically for them.

Make the link

Consumer behaviour is linked to psychology as it attempts to understand how people behave.

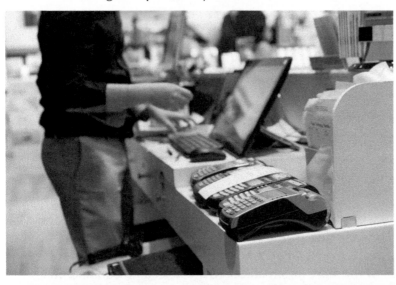

Individual activity

Ask people in your class and/or at home to make a list of products they buy:

- routinely
- on impulse
- only after lots of thought.

Find out the reasons for buying these different products under these different circumstances.

Skills

- Applying

? Questions

1. Describe four methods of market segmentation.
2. Give three differences between product-led and market-led.
3. What is the difference between differentiated and undifferentiated marketing?
4. Suggest two reasons why businesses are interested in consumer behaviour.
5. Suggest four questions that a business might consider when studying consumer behaviour.
6. Describe different types of purchases.
7. Describe features of an EPOS system.

Market research

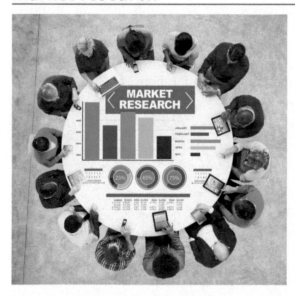

⚠ Watch point

You need to be able to explain how market research can enhance the effectiveness of a business.

Market research aims to find out what customers want and what is happening in the marketplace. It involves looking at what already exists (secondary information) and finding out something new (primary information). Market research can find out:

- the types of customers who are making purchases and their buying habits

- how successful marketing and advertising campaigns are, and whether or not they are cost effective

- what changes might need to be made to existing products to improve them

- what customers would like to see in the future

⚠ Watch point

Field and research are TYPES of market research (not METHODS).

- how customers have reacted to, for example, different products, prices and promotions.

There are two types of market research: field and desk.

Field research

This involves carrying out research to gather new information. As this information is gathered first-hand for a specific purpose, it is called **primary information**.

Field research methods include:

⠶ Make the link

Surveys/questionnaires and interviews could be carried out electronically. For example, using Microsoft Forms for surveys/questionnaires and using Skype for interviews.

- surveys/questionnaires

- interviews

- observations

- hall tests

- focus groups

Desk research

This involves looking at existing information (**secondary information**) from either within the organisation (**internal information**) or outwith the organisation (**external information**).

Desk research might involve looking at:

- websites
- newspaper articles and magazines
- government reports
- textbooks.

Make the link

All research has to be carried out ethically. A business has to make sure that it respects people's views, privacy and right not to take part.

Sources of information

	Benefits	Costs
Primary	• Source is known and is therefore more reliable than secondary information. • Information is gathered for a specific purpose and is therefore relevant.	• Time consuming to collect, which might delay decision-making. • Expensive to collect, which will reduce profitability.
Secondary	• Easier to obtain than primary information. • Usually cheaper to obtain than primary information.	• It was collected for another purpose so might not be as useful. • The information might be biased, which would lead to wrong decisions being made.
Internal	• Unique to the organisation and is therefore relevant. • The source is known and therefore more reliable.	• Information might not be up-to-date or complete, which means a wrong decision could be made. • Computer systems might be required to store internal information, which would be expensive.
External	• Easy to obtain, saving the organisation time. • More information can be accessed through, for example, the internet compared to internal information.	• Source might not be known and could be unreliable. • The information might not be up-to-date, meaning it might not be relevant anymore.

Field research methods

Questionnaire/survey

A survey (questionnaire) involves asking people their views and opinions through a series of questions. It could be done in person, over the telephone, through the post or, more commonly, online, as well as on the street. Sometimes people might be asked for their general views on something or they might be asked to rate a certain thing, e.g. how much they agree or disagree with something.

⚠ Watch point

You may carry out field research as part of your Course Assessment.

Questionnaires are relatively inexpensive to carry out compared to other methods of field research and large numbers of people are usually able to take part. However, people do not always like filling in surveys and they might not always give an honest answer.

Survey Method	Benefits	Costs
Personal Interview This is a face-to-face interview. A number of questions will be asked by the interviewer.	• Clarification can be gained on questions not understood. • Body language and facial expression can be monitored. • Information is obtained instantly.	• Time consuming and expensive to carry out. • Not many people may be able to be interviewed in this way compared to other survey methods. • Researcher requires training to be successful (e.g. questioning techniques).
Telephone Survey People are contacted by telephone and asked to answer questions.	• People spread across large geographical areas can be accessed. • Less expensive than a personal interview. • Clarification can be obtained. • Information is obtained instantly.	• People might not like taking part in a telephone survey. • Large and/or time-consuming surveys are unlikely to be suitable for this method.
Postal Survey A survey is sent through the post, is completed and then sent back.	• People spread across large geographical areas can be accessed. • Surveys can be completed at a time that people choose and is more convenient to them.	• Relies on people opening the letter containing the questionnaire in the first place, completing it and sending it back. • Information is not obtained instantly. • Clarification cannot be gained; the survey has to be designed carefully.
Online Survey A website (e.g. through 'Survey Monkey' or social media) is used to ask questions and people simply access the website to answer them.	• Online software can often be free of charge. • No postal or telephone costs. • People spread across large geographical areas and countries can be accessed. • Online software can often collect and analyse the results.	• Online software that is free might limit the number of questions that can be asked. • People require access to the internet. • Clarification cannot be gained; the survey has to be designed carefully.
Street Survey Asking people in the street to complete a survey.	• Specific individuals can be chosen (e.g. based on their age or gender). • Clarification can be gained.	• Expensive to carry out as individuals need to be employed to carry out the survey.

Observations

An observation involves watching something and then recording what happens. It might be that the observer is counting the number of times something happens or someone does something, or what someone's reaction is to a particular situation.

Benefits	Costs
• Numerical information (quantitative information) is gathered, which is easier to analyse than people's views or opinions (qualitative information). • Often, people are unaware that they are being observed so should act naturally.	• Those being observed cannot be asked for their opinion as to why they did or did not do something. • Observers need to be trained in carrying out observations.

Hall tests

A hall test involves a product being given to customers to try and then their opinions on it obtained. It allows for first-hand information about the product to be obtained and is relatively inexpensive to carry out. However, people might not be honest about what they think about the product as they have tried it for free.

Focus groups

A focus group is a discussion between a selected number of people and a researcher. People will be asked for their views on certain topics and the idea is to generate a discussion around these topics. It allows the business to gain an understanding of people's feelings, but this information can be difficult to analyse.

Sampling

When field research is being carried out, it is impossible to ask everyone for their opinions on something. Because of this, people have to be selected to take part in a piece of research. Different sampling methods can be used to select people to take part in research.

- **Random sampling** – randomly selecting people from a list, e.g. a telephone directory. These individuals must then be questioned. It limits interviewer bias as they have not selected particular individuals to participate.

- **Quota sampling** – selecting people to question based on certain characteristics, e.g. age, gender or occupation. The interviewer simply selects those who meet the given characteristic, but this can lead to bias. It is less expensive to carry out than random sampling.

GO! Group activity

Using an electronic survey package (e.g. Microsoft Forms or SurveyMonkey), create a survey for your class or people in your school to complete on one of the following topics:

- Quality of food in the school canteen.

- Facilities in your school.

- The ways your school is socially responsible.

Once you have created your survey, think about the sampling strategy you are going to use. Then, issue your survey to your sample and wait for people to complete it. Once people have completed your survey, you can then analyse the responses and write a short report detailing your conclusions and recommendations. You might want to include some graphs from the information you collected. You should also evaluate the way you carried out your survey and think about how you could do it differently in the future. Make a note of the benefits and costs of using a survey as a method of field research.

Skills

- Writing
- Information handling
- Applying
- Analysing & evaluating

? Questions

1. What is market research?
2. Distinguish between desk and field research.
3. Give three methods of desk research.
4. Give three methods of field research.
5. Give three reasons why market research can enhance the effectiveness of a company.
6. Describe and justify three methods of field research.
7. Distinguish between primary and secondary information.
8. Distinguish between internal and external information.
9. Describe two sampling techniques.
10. Suggest two ways ICT could be used as part of the market research process.

Desk research methods

Desk research involves looking at different types of secondary (existing) information. Some of this information might be available electronically through, for example, the internet. There are different types of information that might be analysed:

- **Written** – information that is presented as text, e.g. reports, text messages, e-mails, written text on web pages.

- **Oral** – information that is spoken and heard by someone else, e.g. in a meeting or on the telephone or from a TV programme.

- **Pictorial** – information presented through photographs or pictures in reports, newspapers or websites.

- **Graphical** – information presented through a graph or chart.

- **Numerical** – information presented through numbers, e.g. sales figures on websites of companies.

Information might be **quantitative**, in that it is factual and can be measured or counted, or it might be **qualitative**, in that it is based on the opinion of someone.

	Benefits	Costs
Written	• Can be kept for future reference. • Facts can be passed on more accurately compared to oral information.	• May be unable to obtain clarification. • Requires a degree of literacy skills.
Oral	• Instant response is given. • Questions can be asked immediately. • Body language can be monitored.	• Points might be misinterpreted. • Requires careful listening skills.
Pictorial	• Information is presented attractively. • Significant points can be highlighted and/or emphasised.	• Complex information cannot be communicated. • Factual information cannot be communicated as easily as in written information.

(*continued*)

Graphical	• Comparisons can be made easily. • Complex information can be presented clearly.	• Requires numeracy skills to create graphs. • The user needs to be able to interpret graphical information.
Numerical	• Financial information can be analysed. • Calculations can be carried out.	• Requires numeracy skills to handle and interpret numerical information.

 Make the link

Good literacy and numeracy skills are required to handle different types of research.

 Individual activity

Create a mind map that:

• outlines different methods of market research

• identifies the benefits and costs of each one

• gives an example of when each method could be used.

You can create your mind map on paper or using mind mapping software.

Skills

• Applying

• Analysing & evaluating

The extended marketing mix

The basic marketing mix consists of the **4 Ps** – product, price, place and promotion. Organisations must get the balance between different elements of the marketing mix correct in order to be successful.

At National 5, we explored what each element of the marketing mix is as well as why it is important. Before moving on, you should revise the following topics:

• branding

• product development

• factors to be considered before setting a price

• factors to be considered when choosing a business location

• distribution methods (road, rail, air, sea)

• advertising and promotion methods.

 Revision activity

Download and complete the revision sheet from the Leckie & Leckie website. This looks at market segments, branding and product development.

Because organisations are now so closely focused on their customers, the extended marketing mix (or service marketing mix) is commonly being used and is made up of 7 Ps. The extended marketing mix consists of the basic marketing mix with an additional 3 Ps:

- **Process** – the different processes and systems used to deliver the service being provided.

- **People** – those involved in providing the service to customers, e.g. staff.

- **Physical evidence** – the location of where the service is being offered and what it looks like, e.g. store layout and design. It also considers the layout and design of the organisation's website.

Process is important because customers expect the service they receive to be efficient and reliable. For example, when you place an order at a fast food 'drive thru' counter, you expect to receive the order within a very short period of time. The fast food establishment has to have a process in place to make this happen. New ways of providing a service have to be offered to customers through, for example, smartphones and tablet computers. The information customers receive through, for example, a website needs to be kept up-to-date and should be user friendly. (NB the layout and accessibility of a website would be considered under physical evidence.) Businesses have to keep monitoring their processes and updating them where necessary to make sure customers receive what they expect. Customer impressions count!

People is important because customers expect to receive a high quality service. Making sure the correct people are employed and then trained is important in achieving this. Rewarding them and encouraging them to work hard is also important. The organisation should promote a culture of good customer care and have customer care policies in place covering handling customer queries, after-sales service and complaints.

Physical evidence is important because it helps a customer to distinguish one organisation from another. It includes the layout, design and facilities available within a store or where the service is being provided. In a supermarket, the fixtures and fittings within the store will create an impression as well as the signage and facilities available. A hotel user will judge the physical evidence of the quality of the bed provided as well as the facilities that the hotel has to offer; for example, swimming pool and restaurant. Customers are unlikely to purchase from a business if physical evidence is poor, e.g. you wouldn't buy

GO! Paired activity

Choose an organisation that you are familiar with, e.g. a local shop.
For each element of the extended marketing mix, think about how your organisation could change it to improve its effectiveness. You should also think about the costs and benefits of the changes you are suggesting. Put your findings in a discussion board for others to read and comment on.

Skills

- Applying
- Analysing & evaluating

Watch point

Make sure you can explain how each element of the marketing mix can be changed in order to improve the effectiveness of an organisation.

 Group activity

Choose a company and analyse the layout of its website and/or mobile phone app. Think about:

- Layout and design; use of space, colour, images and graphics.
- How easy is it to find the information customers might want?
- What improvements could be made to make the website or app easier to navigate?

Skills

- Applying
- Analsying & evaluating

meat from a counter in a supermarket that was dirty! The atmosphere, mood and feel of the company's physical evidence (the 'ambience') is also important, as it leaves the customer with a certain impression of the business. The layout, design and accessibility of a website or app is also part of physical evidence. These need to be designed in a way to allow customers to easily navigate their way through them and to find what they are looking for.

❓ Questions

1. Give a reason why businesses have to consider the extended marketing mix.
2. Describe the three additional elements of the extended marketing mix.
3. Give an example of each element of the extended marketing mix.
4. Suggest ways each element of the extended marketing mix could be changed to enhance the effectiveness of a business.

Product

Product is the actual (good or service) product being sold.

Product is important because customers won't buy something they don't want; market research identifies what customers want. The more products that are sold, the more chance the business will have of maximising sales.

An organisation can change the product by bringing out a new one or making an adaptation to an existing product. This will invite new people to try it and will help to maintain existing customer loyalty.

At National 5, we looked at the different activities that take place before a product is launched onto the market. We also looked at the basic product life cycle (introduction, growth, maturity and decline). At Higher, we need to build on this by looking at:

- the six-stage product life cycle
- sales and profitability at each stage of the product life cycle
- ways of extending the product life cycle
- product portfolio.

Product life cycle

The product life cycle has six stages: development, introduction, growth, maturity, saturation and decline.

⚠ **Watch point**

If you have time in an exam, a correctly drawn and labelled product life cycle can sometimes gain you marks.

Stage	Description	Sales and profitability
Development	Research and development of the product. A number of activities are carried out (e.g. market research, test marketing, a prototype is built). *Please revise product development from National 5.*	No sales, high costs. No profit.
Introduction	Product is launched onto the market. Product is heavily advertised and sales will begin to increase.	Sales are low and costs are high. Very little, if no, profit.
Growth	The product has gained greater awareness and sales grow rapidly.	Sales grow rapidly and profit begins to increase.
Maturity	Sales are at a peak and the product is well known in the marketplace. Extension strategies might be used at this stage to keep sales at a peak.	High sales and high profits.
Saturation	The end of maturity; everyone has the product and is no longer demanding it. This might be a single point of time or it might be for longer.	Sales and profits are high before they begin to decrease.
Decline	Sales decline as newer and better products are introduced to the market. The product is no longer wanted. Product is eventually withdrawn.	Sales are declining. Profits fall and a loss might be incurred eventually.

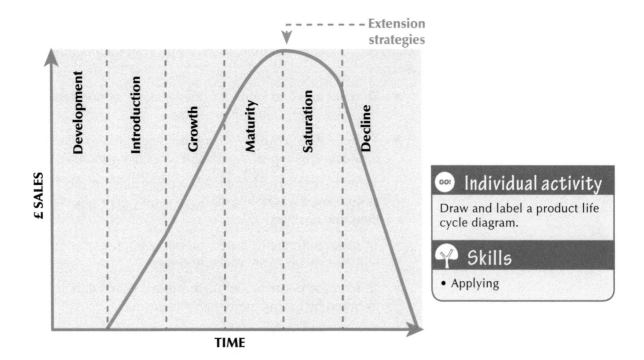

GO! Individual activity

Draw and label a product life cycle diagram.

Skills
• Applying

Group activity

Find examples of products that are at different stages of the product life cycle. Make a list of different extension strategies that have been used to inject new life into some of these products. Think about how successful, or not, these extension strategies have been and why.
Be prepared to present your findings to the rest of your class.

 Skills

- Applying
- Analysing & evaluating

 Group activity

Do some research and find three examples of a product that had an extension strategy introduced.
Note down:
- What the extension strategy is.
- The possible benefits and costs of the extension strategy.

Skills

- Applying
- Analysing & evaluating

Extension strategies

An organisation wants to keep its product at the maturity stage for as long as possible. This is because the product is most profitable at this stage. To do this, they have to inject new life into the product to keep it selling. They do this by introducing **extension strategies** to the product:

- Changing the appearance of the packaging to give the product a new image.
- Changing the size, variety or shape of the product, as this makes it different from the original.
- Improving the quality of the finished product by, for example, using higher quality raw materials.
- Changing the method of promotion used to promote the product; for example, by offering a discount.
- Changing the method of advertising the product to reach a larger number of people.
- Changing the price of the product (up or down) to reach a different market segment.
- Changing the place the product is sold; for example, offering it online as well as in a shop.
- Changing the name of the product.
- Changing the use of the product so that it can be used for different purpose.

Product portfolio

Many organisations sell more than one product for a number of reasons:

- To reduce risk of failure of one product, as one product might be doing better than another.
- To appeal to a variety of market segments, as different products will appeal to different types of customers.
- To increase sales and profits from selling different products, as customers will be able to buy a variety of products from the same business.
- To make introducing a new product easier, as customers will already be aware of the business.
- To increase awareness of the business, its reputation and its brand by having more than one product.
- To cope with products that are only demanded in certain seasons, as other products will gain sales at different times of the year.

Boston Matrix

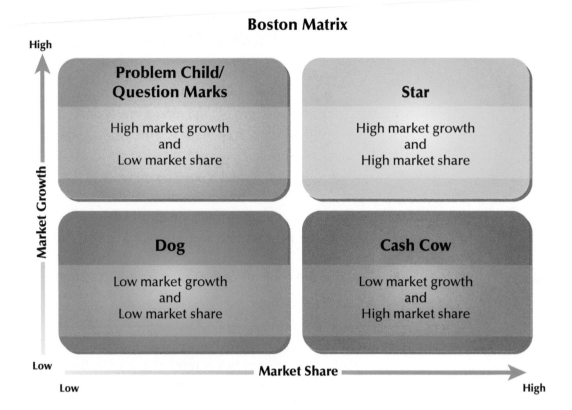

A Boston Matrix (or Boston Box) is often used to plot the range of products that an organisation offers. It can help the organisation to identify where products might need to be introduced or changed.

An organisation will try to have as many 'star' products as possible and will focus its marketing activities to try and achieve this.

There are some costs of having a varied product portfolio:

- Costs of promoting and advertising lots of different products could be high and could result in less profit.

- If one product receives a bad reputation or image this might impact on all the products being sold by the business.

- Maintaining a varied product portfolio will involve a high cost of research and development.

- Cost of purchasing and maintaining machinery for different types of products might be high.

- Staff may require training on the features of different products; which could be time consuming and expensive.

> ⚠ **Watch point**
>
> You need to be able to describe the benefits and costs of having a varied product portfolio.

? Questions

1. Define the term 'product'.
2. Describe the six stages of the product life cycle.
3. Describe profitability at each stage of the product life cycle.
4. What are extension strategies?
5. Describe and justify ways a business can extend the life of a product.
6. Define what is meant by the term 'product portfolio'.
7. Suggest two benefits and two costs of a varied product portfolio.
8. Describe the contents of the Boston matrix.

Price

Price is how much is charged for the actual product. It is important because customers will not buy a product if it costs too much. The price must not be too high compared to a competitor and it must reflect the quality of the product. The price charged should enable the business to cover its costs and also to make a profit.

The different factors to be considered before setting a price were covered at National 5. At Higher, we need to look at different pricing strategies.

Pricing strategy	What is it?	Advantages	Disadvantages
Cost-based (cost plus)	Cost of making the product is calculated and then a percentage for profit is added on ('mark-up'). *E.g. if an item costs £5 to make and a mark-up of 50% is added (£2.50), the selling price would be £7.50.*	• Cost of making the product or providing the service is factored into the selling price; thus, costs are covered. • Easy for the business to calculate compared to other methods (e.g. discrimination), which can vary. • The business may feel it can justify an increase in price if costs rise.	• More difficult for the business to respond to changes in demand compared to e.g. discrimination pricing. • Cost of production may be based on an estimate as actual costs of e.g. energy may be unknown.

(continued)

Skimming	Price is initially set high and will then reduce over time. *E.g. a new mobile phone might be set at £500 for the first couple of months and then gradually decrease in price.*	• Those keen to buy the product when it is first launched will be prepared to pay the high price. • Initial costs of making the product can be recovered early because a high price is charged (and high profit obtained). • As price decreases, customers on a lower income will be able to purchase the product.	• Pricing strategy not so effective for products with lots of competition as customers may choose to buy from them. • Customers on a lower income cannot initially afford to buy the product. • Customers who paid the initial high price might feel unhappy.
Penetration	A low price is initially set and will increase over time. *E.g. low charges for broadband for the first 3 months, which then increases over time.*	• Awareness of the product or service can be obtained quickly. • Allows a company to enter a competitive market and gain market share by having customers switch to them. • As prices increase over time, this allows the company to increase its profits.	• Costs might not be covered initially and therefore a loss is achieved. • Involves a high degree of risk as customers who are loyal to other companies may not want to move.
Price discrimination	A different price is charged to different groups of customers for the same product. *E.g. discounts for students, discount on rail fares for travelling 'off peak', cheaper air fare if seats left.*	• Allows services to be provided that may otherwise not be (e.g. off peak travel). • Some customers benefit from lower prices (e.g. students). • Demand for a product or service can be managed by varying the price.	• Higher prices can be charged for products or services in demand (e.g. travelling at busy times of the day). • Customers may view the pricing strategy as unfair. • Costs of administering this pricing strategy can be high as the price can change frequently.
Destroyer/ predatory	A very low price is charged with the aim of forcing competitors out of the market.	• A company may be able to force a competitor out of the market who cannot compete with the price charged.	• Costs may not be covered and therefore a loss is achieved.
Loss leaders	The product is priced at a loss.	• Can encourage customers to buy other products, e.g. while shopping in a supermarket. • Loss leaders can be a form of advertising if they are particularly inviting. • Can encourage customers to become loyal to the business.	• A loss is made on the product and this may not be easily recovered. • Competitors may also price the same product as a loss leader and therefore the strategy becomes less effective.

(continued)

Promotional	A lower price than normal is charged for a specific period of time (i.e. a discount is given). *E.g. Black Friday offers or a company having a sale.*	• Excess inventory can be sold. • Customers may buy other products at the same time as buying the product on promotion.	• Cost of making or providing the good/service may not be covered. • Customers who are unable to purchase a product at the promotional rate may be left unhappy.
Psychological	The price charged gives the customer an impression the product is much cheaper than it actually is. *E.g. 99p rather than £1.00.*	• Encourages customers to buy the product as it is viewed as being good value.	• As this is now a popular pricing strategy, its effectiveness is not as good as it used to be. • If used all the time by a company, customers will expect all of its products to be priced in this way.

⚠ Watch point

As well as being able to describe different strategies, make sure you can justify why they would be used.

Which price?

Businesses need to think carefully about which price to charge. Certain pricing strategies are only for the short term, whereas some are for the long term.

Market skimming, for example, can be used as strategies for unique and exclusive products. This is because these strategies demand a higher price and consumers associate this with high quality. In competitive markets, destroyer pricing could be used in the hope that it will remove competition in the market, allowing an organisation to increase its market share and also the price of the product in the long term.

Some organisations can charge high prices because other factors will contribute to their success; for example, their product being unique, little competition, brand loyalty or limited supply.

A business has to constantly review the price it charges because it operates in an environment that does not stand still. Changes in demand because of external factors are common, as is pressure from customers to lower prices. Competitors are also doing their market research and trying to introduce products that will be better and cheaper than their rivals.

😊 Individual activity

You have been asked to give advice to someone who is setting up their own business. They are confused by the different pricing strategies available and when they might be used.

Create a factsheet or leaflet describing different types of pricing strategies that are available to organisations and when they might be used. Use desktop publishing or word processing software to create your factsheet/leaflet.

🌳 Skills

- Applying
- Analysing & evaluating

? Questions

1. What is price?
2. Justify the use of the following pricing strategies:
   - destroyer
   - skimming
   - psychological
   - discrimination
   - cost-plus
3. Suggest and justify a pricing strategy that might be used for a new product.
4. Suggest and justify a pricing strategy that might be used for a product with an exclusive image.
5. Describe factors needing to be taken into account when deciding on which pricing strategy to use.
6. Suggest reasons why a business has to constantly review its prices.

Place

Place is about getting the product to the customer and where it is sold. Changes to where the product can be bought and how it gets to the customer may attract new customers.

Channels of distribution

Channel of distribution is the route a product will follow to get from the manufacturer to the customer. The route always starts with the manufacturer and ends with the customer. The four channels of distribution are shown above.

There are a number of factors that will determine which channel of distribution is used. These factors include:

- The actual product and its life cycle (products with a shorter life cycle may need to be sold directly to the customer to preserve them, e.g. fresh fruit or flowers).

- The image and exclusivity the manufacturer wants the product to have.

- The availability of finance.

- The reputation and reliability of wholesalers and retailers.

- Legal restrictions.

- The logistic facilities available to the manufacturer (their ability to transport and store the product from one place to the next).

Wholesalers

A wholesaler buys large quantities of items from the manufacturer and then sells them on to retailers, or directly to the customer, in smaller quantities. Many larger retailers do not use a wholesaler as part of their distribution channel because they have their own warehouses and transport systems (this is sometimes referred to as 'logistics', see page 103).

Make the link

The method of physical distribution (e.g. road, rail, air and sea) was covered at National 5.

💡 Revision activity

Download and complete the revision sheet from the Leckie & Leckie website. This looks at methods of physical distribution.

The use of a wholesaler has costs and benefits.

Benefits	Costs
• Distribution and storage costs are reduced because products might be bought in bulk. • The wholesaler may promote the manufactured product, resulting in less cost for the manufacturer. • The risk of not selling the product to a retailer or to the customer is taken on by the wholesaler and therefore risk for the manufacturer is reduced. • Packaging, labelling and marketing might be carried out by the wholesaler. • The manufacturer does not have to worry about having to sell excess inventory if there are changes in the business environment (e.g. fashion). • The wholesaler may provide information on the product for the retailer. • Retailers do not have to pay for expensive storage facilities to hold inventory as they can buy smaller quantities compared to sourcing directly from the manufacturer.	• The manufacturer loses control over what happens to the product after they have sold it and may not like the way the product is being portrayed by wholesalers or retailers. • There is less profit for the manufacturer as they have not sold directly to the customer. • Loyalty and any associated benefits of this (e.g. discounts with the manufacturer) cannot be gained.

Retailers

A retailer is an organisation that distributes products to the customer on behalf of the manufacturer. Retailers stock a range of products from a number of manufacturers and wholesalers. The retailer will decide on the price to be charged to the customer and how to display the product to be sold. The manufacturer will decide which retailer to use based on where the customers are and what extra services (e.g. credit and delivery terms) they offer the customer.

Make the link

The changing business environment influences the popularity and growth of different retailers. There has been a change in retailing trends over the past several years.

Retailers benefit from sourcing products directly from a manufacturer because they can tell them what quantity they want and at what cost; larger retailers (e.g. supermarkets) may be particularly powerful at being able to specify what they want. Sometimes retailers can take advantage of economies of scale (the benefits of buying in bulk). Sometimes manufacturers will decide not to use a retailer as part of the channel of distribution because the product will face competition in store from other manufacturers' products and because it adds on an extra financial cost to the distribution channel.

Types of retailers

Supermarkets	Often very large organisations that buy large quantities and then sell them in their stores. They mainly supply food and drink but have increasingly started to supply other products such as electrical and home wares. Local supermarkets (e.g. Tesco Express) are growing in popularity. Large supermarkets have put many smaller businesses (e.g. corner shops) out of business in some towns.
Discount retailer	They tend to provide non-branded products at a cheap price. These types of stores have become very popular in the UK because of the economic climate. The growth of them has resulted in other retailers having to discount their own products in order to remain competitive.
E-tailer	Shopping online and having the product delivered to you (e.g. through Amazon). This type of retailer often has lower overhead costs because they do not have to worry about having stores from which to sell their products. However, they often require large warehouses to store their products. They may rely on different logistic companies to distribute their products.
Convenience retailer	Often referred to as the corner shop. This type of retailer normally has a small shop where a limited amount of products can be bought. They are often found in busy residential areas and are normally more expensive than supermarkets. This is because they do not have the same buying power as supermarkets and because they are offering a product in a convenient place for their customer.

Direct selling

Internet selling (or e-tailing) involves selling products to the customer through an internet website. S-commerce, using social media, is also popular. An internet website is a collection of information in one place that can be seen by typing in a website address (a URL) into a browser such as Internet Explorer or Safari. An organisation may have a website to sell its products and also to advertise them.

Benefits	Costs
• Customers worldwide can purchase goods. • Customers can buy online 24/7 from their own home. • Online discounts may be available as a shop is not required. • Product information can be updated and accessed quickly. • Products can be compared with others. • Convenient if access to a retailer is not available. • Inventory availability can often be checked instantly and products reserved. • A website can be set up fairly cheaply.	• The customer is unable to see or handle the goods before purchasing. • Customers might not want to provide their credit or debit card details to a website. • Internet or computer problems might occur when ordering. • There is a time delay between ordering and actually receiving the good. • Items can get lost or damaged during transportation. • There is no personal contact with the organisation. • Relies on customers being able to use a computer and navigate around a website. • A web designer may be required to create a high quality website and this might be expensive.

Paired activity

Think about your local high street or town. Create a list of the different types of retailers that exist. Use Google Maps to help you.

Skills

• Applying

Personal selling involves a trained sales member of the organisation selling the product directly to the customer. You commonly see it in shopping centres as you walk through. It allows the sales member to demonstrate how the product works to the customer and to answer any questions that they may have. Customers might feel pressured into buying the product and this might put them off. It also requires training to be given to ensure the sales member is knowledgeable about the product and how it works.

Direct mail involves posting letters or leaflets directly to the homes of potential customers. This allows for specific market segments to be targeted, covering large geographical areas. However, customers might not like receiving lots of mail in this way and might just bin it (we all know how frustrating 'junk mail' can be).

Mail order, buying through a catalogue, is another method of direct selling. It is convenient to the customer as they can look

Make the link

Direct mail can also be sent via e-mail and is cheaper than sending letters or leaflets through the post.

through the catalogue in their own time and order when they feel ready. It also reduces the costs associated with having expensive high street stores. However, catalogues can be expensive to produce and are not environmentally friendly; they might not fit in with having the aim of being socially responsible. The customer receives no personal attention from the organisation and the time they might have to wait to receive their order might also put them off.

TV shopping channels are another example of direct selling.

? Questions

1. Describe 'channels of distribution'.
2. Suggest factors to take into account when deciding on which channel of distribution to use.
3. Distinguish between a wholesaler and a retailer.
4. Describe two benefits and two costs of using a wholesaler.
5. Describe two benefits and two costs of using a retailer.
6. Describe different types of retailers.
7. Give examples of different types of retailers.
8. Define the term 'logistics'.
9. Describe the methods of direct selling.
10. For each method given in Q9, suggest two benefits and two costs of that method.

☀ Revision activity

Download and complete the revision sheet from the Leckie & Leckie website. This looks at methods of promotion.

Make the link

Technology can be used in a variety of ways in promotion.

Promotion

Promotion lets people know that a product exists and tries to encourage them to buy it. This is important because customers need to be informed that a product is available. Advertising is a part of promotion but it isn't the only part of it.

Above and below the line

Promotion is often described as above or below the line.

- **Above the line promotion** – mass media promotions to a large range of people; for example, through social media, newspapers, posters, TV and cinema adverts, radio advertising, billboards and other forms of mass media advertising.

- **Below the line promotion** – promotions to focused groups of people; for example, sales promotions, public relations and direct selling.

Above the line promotion

At National 5, various forms of above the line promotions were covered and you should go back and revise these carefully. Make sure you are able to describe different methods as well as being able to explain the benefits and costs of each. *These are all thoroughly covered in the National 5 Course Notes.* Technology is playing a major role in above the line promotions through, for example, internet websites, social media, e-mail and mobile applications.

Celebrities might also be used to promote a business. This is known as **celebrity** or **product endorsement**.

Benefits	Costs
• Promotes a good image and name for the organisation. • People often want to buy products to be associated with the celebrity. • If the celebrity is successful, it can increase sales levels.	• Celebrities are expensive to pay. • The celebrity has to be carefully chosen to match the image the product needs to have. • Negative publicity about the celebrity can impact negatively on sales of the product.

Below the line promotion

Special offers or sales promotions might include discounts on buying a product, free samples or a free gift when you purchase something. They are usually on offer for a limited period of time and try to encourage people to buy the product. For example, magazines usually give free gifts away when they are first launched as well as being at a reduced price to encourage people to buy them. Loyalty cards are another example of sales promotions.

Public relations (PR) attempts to improve the relationship and communication between the general public and an organisation. Large organisations may have a PR office or department that has responsibility for organising different PR events. Effective PR will give the organisation a good image, which in turn can increase sales. PR activities include:

Press releases	A press release is usually a written statement to the press (e.g. newspapers and TV stations) that communicates activities within the organisation.
Sponsorships	Organisations may sponsor events where there is likely to be a lot of public attention. Sport and charity events are often sponsored by large organisations that have their company name displayed on material that the sport or charity is distributing. Football strips sponsored by companies are a good example.
Charity donations	Organisations may donate sums of money to charities in the hope of not only helping a good cause, but also being seen as socially responsible. This will raise awareness of the organisation.

Into and out of the pipeline

Manufacturer

Into the pipeline

Retailer

Retailers encourage customers to buy from them; for example, free samples, loyalty schemes, credit facilities, demonstrations, competitions, offers such as BOGOF and vouchers.

Manufacturers encourage retailers to stock their products; for example, point of sale materials, dealer loaders, sale or return, competitions, staff training and credit facilities.

Out of the pipeline

Customer

Into the pipeline promotions	Out of the pipeline promotions
Point of sale materials Often free posters, display standards and other material are given to retailers to display products to customers.	**Free samples** Customers are given small samples of the product free of charge so that they can see/test the product in the hope they will buy it.
Sale or return The manufacturer gives the retailer the opportunity to return products to reduce the risk of being stuck with inventory that has not sold.	**Loyalty schemes** Many larger retailers offer loyalty schemes to customers whereby they collect points for making purchases. These points can then be used to obtain vouchers for discount on future purchases or for free admission/discounts for visitor attractions.
Staff training The manufacturer may provide training and demonstrations to the retailer's staff so that they feel confident in promoting the manufacturer's product.	**Vouchers** These are usually given in newspapers/magazines in store. They entitle the customer to a discount on purchases they make at a later date.
Dealer (retailer) loaders These are offers given to encourage the retailer to stock the manufacturer's products (e.g. buy so many and get one free).	**Special offers** For example, buy one get one free (BOGOF) and other reductions in the price of a product. They are usually short-term and only on selected products.

Marketing and ethics

The **Advertising Standards Authority** monitors advertising and other forms of promotion to ensure they are to the required standard. They also investigate any advertising-related complaints. They have the authority to enforce changes to adverts or promotions if they contain wrong or misleading information.

? Questions

1. Distinguish between above and below the line promotions.
2. Distinguish between into and out of the pipeline promotions.
3. Describe two methods each of above and below the line promotions.
4. For each method given in Q3, describe two benefits and two costs.
5. Describe two methods each of into and out of the pipeline promotions.
6. For each method given in Q5, describe two benefits and two costs.
7. Describe the role of public relations.
8. Describe methods of public relations.
9. Suggest ways technology can be used in promotional activities.

★ Key questions

1. Explain ways market research can be used to enhance the effectiveness of large organisations.
2. Explain ways the marketing mix can be used to enhance the effectiveness of large organisations.
3. Describe the costs and benefits of a large organisation having a varied product portfolio.
4. Describe ways current technologies can be used in marketing.

Summary

This chapter introduced you to the importance of the customer and customer behaviour. Each element of the extended marketing mix was explored and why each element is important. Two types of market research (desk and field) were explored, and the various methods of market research that can be used covered. Throughout the chapter, examples of how technology can be used in marketing were provided.

The main topics in this chapter were:

- Customers
- Market research
- Extended marketing mix
- Technology in marketing

By successfully answering the key questions, you will show that you have grasped the main topics covered in this chapter.

3 END OF CHAPTER MATERIAL

Sample exam question

Make sure you read each exam question carefully as every word is there for a reason. It is good practice to break each question down into parts before you answer it so that you know what is required.

For example:

⚠ Watch point

You must write your answer according to the command word(s) used in the question. In this explain question, you need to give a reason why something is a benefit.

- **Explain the benefits of a mobile application (app) in promotion. (3 marks)**

The command word – NB explain is more than just describe!

Only benefits are required – not costs.

Your answer must be specific to promotion.

Sample answer

Customers can access the app at anytime and anywhere (assuming they have a signal), therefore products can be promoted 24/7 by the business **(1 explanation mark)**. Customers across the world can use the app, therefore a larger number of customers can be targeted by the promotion **(1 explanation mark)**. Changes to product information or the selling price can be made quickly, which means customers are kept up-to-date **(1 explanation mark)**.

⚠ Watch point

Use words such as 'therefore' or 'which means' to connect the different parts to your answer in an explain question.

Examiner's comments

The candidate has given three explanation points. Remember, in an explain question that asks for benefits and/or costs, candidates must give a reason why something is a cost or benefit to gain the mark. This is what makes an explain question different (and more difficult!) than a describe question. **(3/3 marks)**

More sample exam questions

- Describe the purpose of marketing activities. (3 marks)
- Describe and justify elements of the extended marketing mix. (6 marks)
- Discuss the role of technology in promotion. (6 marks)
- Explain the importance of carrying out market research. (4 marks)
- Describe and justify methods of field research. (8 marks)
- Compare methods of sampling. (2 marks)
- Describe into and out of the pipeline promotions. (6 marks)
- Describe sales and profitability levels at different stages of the product life cycle. (6 marks)
- Explain the benefits of a varied product portfolio. (6 marks)
- Explain the benefits and costs of four pricing strategies. (8 marks)
- Discuss the role of ethics in marketing. (3 marks)

Check your progress

	NEED HELP	GETTING THERE	CONFIDENT
What is marketing?	◯	◯	◯
Customers and consumer behaviour	◯	◯	◯
Field research	◯	◯	◯
Desk research	◯	◯	◯
Product	◯	◯	◯
Price	◯	◯	◯
Place	◯	◯	◯
Promotion	◯	◯	◯
People	◯	◯	◯
Process	◯	◯	◯
Physical evidence	◯	◯	◯
Technology in marketing	◯	◯	◯

4 Management of Operations

From National 5 you should already be able to:

- Describe factors to consider when choosing a suitable supplier.
- Describe consequences of over- or under-stocking for an organisation.
- Describe factors to consider when choosing a suitable production method.
- Outline methods of ensuring high quality in production practices.
- Outline how technology can be used to contribute to effective operational activity.

What you will learn about in this chapter:

- Inventory management.
- Methods of production.
- Quality.
- Ethical and environmental.
- Technology in operations.

Inventory management

The term inventory refers to raw materials, goods that are currently being manufactured (work in progress) and finished goods. At all stages of the production process inventory must be managed because there must be sufficient quantities of raw materials and finished goods at all times.

At National 5, we explored what factors would be taken into account when choosing a supplier. You should go back and revise this carefully if you need to.

💡 Revision activity

Download and complete the revision sheet from the Leckie & Leckie website. This looks at factors influencing the choice of a supplier.

When manufacturing and storing goods there are different factors to consider:

- The quantity of the product that is required.

- The volume of products that can be manufactured at any one time.

- Working practices, procedures and health and safety requirements.

- The storage available in a warehouse.

- Procedures for maintaining and managing quality.

Organisations need to calculate the **optimum** or **economic inventory level**. This is the most suitable quantity of inventory at any one time. This ensures that costs are kept to a minimum as well as having enough inventory to meet production requirements. The purpose of an inventory management system is to:

- ensure inventory is readily available at any one time

- ensure production continues

- avoid delays to customer orders

- ensure over-stocking does not take place, which results in higher costs

- avoid inventory deteriorating (e.g. fresh food) and/or becoming obsolete.

There are consequences of holding too little or too much inventory.

Consequences of too little inventory	Consequences of too much inventory
- Production could stop and therefore employees and machines sit idle. - Customers might not receive their orders on time, which could result in complaints. - The business could gain a poor reputation and image.	- Increased financial costs (e.g. storage, security and insurance). - Inventory could go to waste or deteriorate, resulting in inventory that needs to be discarded. - Higher risk of inventory being stolen.

Organisations need to have in place an inventory management system to manage inventory levels. An inventory management system has the following features:

- **Maximum inventory level** – the highest amount of inventory that can be stored at one time. At this level, inventory costs will be at the minimum per unit because the organisation is at full capacity.

- **Minimum inventory level** – the lowest amount of inventory that should be stored at one time. At this level, there is a danger that inventory levels could fall too low and production would stop.

- **Buffer inventory** – the inventory used when inventory is below the minimum inventory level to allow production to continue.

- **Re-order level** – the quantity at which more inventory is ordered.

- **Re-order quantity** – the quantity of inventory that has to be ordered to bring levels back to the maximum inventory level.

- **Lead time** – the time that passes between ordering inventory and it arriving.

> ⚠ **Watch point**
>
> Make sure you are able to describe the purpose and the different parts of an inventory management system.

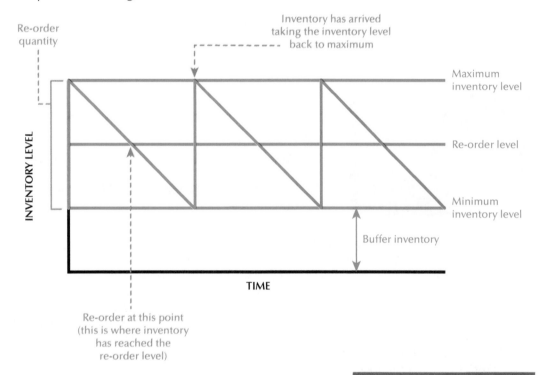

The diagram shows the features of an inventory management system.

Just in time (JIT)

Just in time (JIT) is a method of inventory control that keeps cost levels to the minimum. As the name suggest, inventory arrives *just in time* for it to be used in the production process and goods are only manufactured when a customer order is received.

The benefits of a JIT system are:

- Less cash is tied up in inventory.

- Less storage and warehouse space is required.

> **Watch point**
>
> You can get marks in the exam for being able to draw the inventory management diagram.

- Wastage should be reduced as only inventory required is ordered.

- Changes in the external environment (e.g. fashion trends) will have a reduced impact.

The costs of a JIT system are:

- Suppliers who are reliable are required so that inventory is delivered on time.

- Production can stop if inventory is not delivered when required.

- Less environmentally friendly as more journeys with less inventory will be made.

- Delivery costs might be higher due to more journeys.

- Discounts for bulk buying (economies of scale) might be lost.

Storage and warehousing

Inventory can be stored in a centralised or decentralised location.

- **Centralised storage** – storing inventory in one place.

- **Decentralised storage** – storing inventory in more than one place.

Centralised storage	
Benefits	Costs
• Maintaining security is easier in one location rather than several. • Procedures for receiving, issuing and distributing inventory are easier to implement consistently across the organisation.	• A dedicated central area for storing inventory could be expensive to set up and maintain. • Staff could waste time going to and from the centralised storage area (it might be some distance from their normal location).

Decentralised storage	
Benefits	Costs
• Staff can access inventory more easily rather than having to go to a centralised area. • Less chance of inventory going to waste or deteriorating.	• Storage space in several locations is required. • Security is more difficult to maintain across a number of locations compared to one (and might also be more expensive).

Warehousing

A warehouse is the name given to the place where finished products are held until they are ready to be distributed to the customer. Warehouses need to be designed to ensure the most efficient movement and flow of inventory. The exact size and layout of a warehouse depends on the size of the organisation, the product being manufactured and the organisation's policy for logistics and distribution.

Distribution and logistics

Distribution and logistics is concerned with getting the finished product to the right customer. Channels of distribution were covered earlier (see page 88) and methods of physical distribution were covered at National 5.

How the product gets to the customer depends on the distribution mix. Some organisations may choose to transport the product themselves or they may employ a company that specialises in logistics and distribution to do this. The distribution mix identifies various factors to be considered when deciding upon the route to get the product to the customer.

Factors to consider

- Reliability of other organisations.
- Legal restrictions.
- Availability of finance.
- The product being distributed.
- The image associated with the product.
- The inventory management system being used.
- The distribution capability of the manufacturer.

⚫⋮ Make the link

A warehouse is part of the channel of distribution.

? Questions

1. Describe factors to be considered when selecting a supplier.
2. What is the purpose of an inventory management system? Try to include at least four features.
3. Discuss the consequences of having too much inventory.
4. Discuss the consequences of having too little inventory.
5. Describe the features of an inventory management system.
6. Compare centralised and decentralised storage.
7. Describe the features of a JIT system.
8. Describe the benefits and costs of a JIT system.
9. What is a warehouse?
10. Define the term 'logistics'.
11. Suggest factors to be considered when deciding on how to get the product to the customer.

⁂ Make the link

Value is being added to each product as it moves from one stage of production to another.

Methods of production

Businesses have to decide which method of production to use to make their products. They have to think carefully about how to actually turn their inputs into outputs.

When deciding which method to use, there are different factors to think about:

- The actual product being made.
- The quantity of the product that needs to be made.
- The way the business will make sure the product is of a high quality.
- The way inventory is managed.
- The resources available (e.g. staff and machinery).
- The method of distribution.
- The technology available.

There are three main methods of production: **job, batch** and **flow**.

Job production

Job production is when one product is made from start to finish before another one is made. The product is made to the customer's own requirements and this results in a unique or one-off product being made. Products made by job production are usually made by hand by someone who is very skilled at what they are doing.

Examples: wedding cakes, handmade chocolates, pieces of art, sandwich being made to order in a sandwich shop.

Benefits	Costs
• The customer gets exactly what they want and this can increase their satisfaction. • High prices can often be charged because it is a unique/one-off product. • Designs can be changed to suit each customer's own requirements even when production has begun. • Employees experience making a range of products using different skills. • Employees can be motivated by seeing the product being made from start to finish.	• Highly skilled employees are required to make each different product and this can be expensive (labour intensive). • Specialist tools and equipment might be needed that can be expensive to buy. • Can't always buy raw materials in bulk and might miss out on cost savings from bulk buying (economies of scale). • Can take a long time to make a unique product and this might mean the employee loses motivation.

Batch production

Batch production is when one group of identical products are made at any one time. All products in the batch move onto the next stage of production at the same time. Machinery and equipment can be cleaned and/or changed between batches to produce a different product. Batch production is often used when manufacturing a product that comes in different varieties, styles or sizes.

Examples: cakes, newspapers/magazines, bread.

> ⚠ **Watch point**
>
> Make sure you can describe different methods of production, including the benefits and costs of each.

Benefits	Costs
• Batches can be changed to suit the requirements of the customer, which results in higher customer satisfaction. • Raw materials can be bought in bulk, therefore saving money. • Cost savings can be made, as standardised machinery is used. • The need for highly skilled workers is reduced.	• Equipment and employees might not have anything to do between batches, which costs money. • Any mistakes in one item can result in the whole batch being wasted, which costs money and wastes time. • The cost of each item might be high if the batch size is small, therefore the price charged to the customer might be higher. • Employee motivation can be less than with job production, as they carry out the same, often repetitive, task.

Flow production

Flow production (sometimes known as line production) is when parts are added to the product as it moves along the production line. The final product will have been made by the time it reaches the end of the production line. As the product moves along the production line, machinery (e.g. robots) and workers have very specific tasks to do: one might screw something in and one might paint a very specific part before moving on to the next task (this is known as **division of labour**).

Examples: cars/vans, computers and other electrical items.

Benefits	Costs
• Large amounts of identical products are made. • Raw materials can be bought in bulk, saving the business money. • Production often uses lots of machinery (capital intensive) that, compared to humans, can work for longer and without breaks. • Quality can be easily checked at different stages of production.	• The individual customer's requirements cannot be met because each product is identical. • If a fault occurs during production, this can cause the whole production line to stop. • Large demand for products is needed because they are made in large quantities. • Motivation can be low among employees due to the repetitive nature of the work they have to do.

Flow production to manufacture cars

Capital and labour intensive

The quantity of capital (machinery, equipment and technology) or labour used in an organisation determines whether it is **capital** or **labour** intensive.

- **Automation** means that capital has replaced the need for humans to carry out the work required because machines, equipment and technology can do it instead.

- **Mechanisation** means that there is some capital as well as some labour involved in production, e.g. people working the machines.

Labour intensive	
Benefits	**Costs**
• Employees can use their initiative when required. • There is always a supply of labour available (though highly skilled employees might be more difficult to source). • Cheaper than purchasing and maintaining equipment.	• It costs money to recruit, select and train new employees. • The accuracy and the quality of work from person to person can vary.

Capital intensive	
Benefits	**Costs**
• Machines can work 24/7 without the need for breaks. • Machines can produce a consistent and standardised accuracy and quality of work. • Discounts through buying in bulk (economies of scale) can be obtained. • Products can be produced in large quantities.	• Individual customer requirements cannot be met. • Breakdowns can occur, which can be expensive and have significant implications for meeting deadlines and fulfilling customer orders. • Employees become tired and bored of repetitive tasks that might need to be carried out. • Initial set-up costs can be high.

Paired or group activity

Think of a product that is made using job, batch or flow production. Do some research to find out why it is made in this way and the benefits that this has. Try to find out how much labour and capital is used in the production process. Be prepared to present your findings to the rest of your class.

Skills

• Applying
• Analysing & evaluating

 Questions

1. Describe three methods of production.
2. Give an example of each method of production.
3. Describe benefits and costs of each method of production.
4. Compare labour and capital intensive production.
5. Explain benefits and costs of labour intensive production.
6. Explain benefits and costs of capital intensive production.
7. Define the term 'mechanisation'.
8. Define the term 'automation'.

Quality

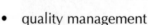

At National 5, we explored the benefits of providing a high quality product as well as some of the methods that can be used to produce a high quality product. At Higher, you need to know about some different methods of ensuring quality:

• quality management
• quality standards and symbols
• benchmarking
• quality circles
• mystery shopping.

 Revision activity

Download and complete the revision sheet from the Leckie & Leckie website. This looks at reasons why quality is important and some methods that can be used to ensure quality.

Quality management

Quality management is one method of ensuring quality. It places a very strong focus on the customer and achieving customer satisfaction. A high level of commitment is required from all staff in order to produce a high-quality product. Staff are also highly skilled and receive regular training. Quality inputs (e.g. raw materials) are required to ensure a quality product is produced. Products are also checked at all stages during production to avoid any product not reaching the required standard and to reduce wastage. There is a focus on the organisation continually trying to improve its products, and the service offered, in order to remain competitive. High-quality products will result in repeat sales and loyal customers as well as the organisation obtaining a good reputation.

Quality standards and symbols

Quality standards are awarded to an organisation when it meets a particular specification or set of criteria. However, it can be a time-consuming process to achieve and involves a series of checks and/ or audits to be carried out. Being awarded a quality standard (or symbol) has benefits to the organisation and the customer.
The organisation benefits from:

- Having a recognised symbol attached to its name, which improves the image and reputation of the product.

- Having proof that it has met specific quality standards.

- Having a competitive advantage over products that do not have a quality standard, which can be used in marketing and promotional material.

- Help to encourage repeat purchases.

- Being able to charge higher prices.

- Receiving fewer complaints and reduced wastage.

Benchmarking

Benchmarking involves comparing one product with another similar product, often using the market leader's standards as the benchmark. The organisation will then attempt to match these standards in their own products.

⚠ Watch point

Methods of ensuring quality is a very common exam question.

GO! Group activity

Research each of the following quality standards/symbols:
- CE marking
- BSI kitemark.
- trade logos.

Find out what they are and when they are used. Try to find some examples of products that carry these quality standards/symbols.

⚲ Skills

- Applying

Benefits	Costs
• Using practices and techniques from those seen to have 'best practice' in the market will improve the performance and image of the organisation and reduce risk. • The organisation can become more competitive. • There is a focus on continual improvement by setting goals, which can motivate employees.	• It takes time and skill to be able to identify and explore practices used by other organisations. • Not all of the information required to decide 'best practice' may be available. • Benchmarking may not be possible due to internal factors (e.g. staffing, availablity of finance or technology).

Quality circles

A quality circle is established when members of the organisation meet to discuss quality issues and then attempt to improve these and find solutions to quality issues. It involves employees at all levels of the hierarchy, which can be motivating. As employees feel empowered, it can improve employee/employer relations and communication between employees and management. Change can also be easier to implement as employees have been involved in the process.

Mystery shopping

Some organisations, often in retail, employ mystery shoppers to visit their store to make a purchase. Feedback is then given to the organisation on how the shopper found their experience and the service that they received. Staff in the organisation will not normally know in advance that a mystery shopper will be visiting, in an attempt to provide an accurate representation of the shop and the service experienced.

 Individual activity

Pretend you are going to be a mystery shopper for a business of your choice. Make a checklist of all the things you would look for if you were a customer of that business. For each point on your checklist, give a reason why it is important.

Skills

• Applying
• Analysing & evaluating

Ethical and environmental

⚡ Make the link

Ethical and environmental issues are related to the objective of social responsibility.

All businesses have to consider environmental and ethical issues. The Government has put in place strict policies and laws that dictate some of the ways businesses have to consider the environment.

Businesses can:

- Try to **minimise wastage** by ensuring employees are trained, ensuring machinery is kept in good condition and by not overstocking. However, providing training and maintaining machinery could be expensive. This would reduce the company's profitability. It is important in maintaining a good reputation that businesses do not simply 'dump' waste materials that could harm the environment, or send all their waste to landfill. They have to make sure that they reduce the amount of waste that is produced as well as ensuring they dispose of it in an environmentally friendly way. Sometimes a business might call on the services of a specialist waste disposal company to dispose of certain types of waste.

- **Recycle as much as possible** by encouraging employees to put rubbish in appropriately coloured bins and by re-using materials in the production process as much as possible. Initially buying the different coloured recycling bins could be expensive, but would hopefully encourage people to recycle as much as they can. Recycling can help reduce the company's energy bill by re-using

GO! Group activity

Find examples in the news of organisations that have been criticised for not operating ethically.

🌱 Skills

- Applying

materials rather than using new ones. Recycling will also help to reduce greenhouse gases by not having to extract new raw materials and by reducing materials that need to be transported.

- **Try to minimise packaging** by only using the amount of packaging needed to maintain the product's quality. Not only will this cut down on costs, it is good for the environment. They also need to try and use as much environmentally friendly packaging that can be recycled as possible; however, it might be more expensive than non-recyclable packaging. Many products that previously had significant amounts of packaging (e.g. Easter eggs) now contain much less.

- **Prevent pollution and emissions** by watching the materials used in production (e.g. fuel and chemicals) and by disposing of any potentially harmful chemicals or products in the most environmentally friendly way. Careful disposal of waste can be expensive, but businesses that don't consider this properly can be prosecuted. Businesses also need to be aware of traffic congestion/pollution getting to and from the business, as well as the noise and light that it emits from its premises.

- **Be sustainable** by replacing raw materials that they have used with new ones. For example, toilet paper manufacturers might plant a new tree for every one that they use to make their product. They might have a sustainable development policy that details what the organisation will do to replace materials that it consumes.

- **Operate a fair trade policy,** which means they only use suppliers that have produced or obtained their raw materials in an ethical manner. The fair trade symbol that is on fair trade products means that those who have produced the product (e.g. farmers) have received a fair price for their product. In addition, the supplier will treat their employees fairly and will have a commitment towards their welfare and health and safety. The fair trade symbol is owned by Fairtrade International and is an independent assurance that the organisation is adopting a fair trade approach to business.

- Ensure animals that are used as part of the product (e.g. eggs) are given a **high standard of animal welfare**. It might also mean that products (e.g. cosmetics) are not tested on animals before they are sold to consumers.

- **Use renewable energy sources** rather than ones that cannot be renewed. This will reduce the impact on the environment.

- **Provide information** on the product that will help consumers make decisions, e.g. nutritional information.

- Adopt **other energy saving strategies** such as energy saving light bulbs, using rain water to flush toilets and solar panels for generating electricity.Make the link

- Avoid using **child labour** in production.

- Ensure **health and safety legislation** is always followed and appropriate training is given.

Group activity

Make a list of the actions your school/college has taken to be environmentally friendly and to operate ethically. Then make a list of recommendations that could be taken to become even more environmentally friendly. Give a reason why each recommendation should be adopted.

Skills

- Applying
- Analysing & evaluating

Paired activity

Visit the Green Choices website (www.greenchoices.org) to find out what you can do to reduce the impact of your daily life on the environment. Try also to think about what businesses could do to reduce their impact.
Be prepared to feed back to the rest of your class.

Skills

- Applying
- Analysing & evaluating

Group activity

Choose an organisation and investigate what strategies it has adopted to reduce the impact it has on the environment. With your findings, prepare a short presentation that provides:
- Some background information on the organisation and what it does.
- Details of how the organisation is protecting the environment.
- The benefits and costs of the strategies it is adopting to protect the environment.
- Recommendations on what the organisation could do to become even more environmentally friendly.

Be prepared to present your findings to the rest of the class.

Skills

- Writing
- Applying
- Analysing & evaluating

Case study

FirstGroup Plc

FirstGroup Plc is committed to protecting the environment. It is a leading transport company and provides bus and rail services across Britain. It has a number of initiatives in place to reduce wastage, increase recycling and protect the environment. It has a section on its website dedicated to corporate social responsibility and ethics.

In 2012, FirstGroup Plc scrapped several hundred buses. Instead of simply sending these to landfill sites, it tried to recycle as many parts as possible. For example, it tried to reuse engines and gearboxes after they had been reconditioned. This required a close relationship between FirstGroup Plc and its suppliers.

FirstGroup Plc has worked with the Salvation Army Trading Company to recycle old uniforms. The Salvation Army Trading Company can sell these to raise income for their charity.

The number of train timetables printed, and the size of these, has been reduced to decrease the volume of emissions from printing and also to limit the volume of paper required to print them. FirstGroup Plc is also encouraging customers to print their own timetables directly from the FirstGroup Plc website.

FirstGroup Plc has a supplier code of conduct that lays down the expectations of its suppliers in terms of their environmental responsibilities.

Questions

1. Suggest reasons why FirstGroup Plc is committed to protecting the environment.
2. From the case study, identify ways that FirstGroup Plc is protecting the environment.
3. For each way identified in Q2, discuss how it would reduce the impact on the environment.

Technology in operations

Technology can be used in a number of different ways in the operations function.

- Computer facilities (e.g. computer and internet) can be used for purchasing materials online.

- E-mail can be used to confirm an order has been received and to let the customer know about the progress and status of the order (e.g. when it has been dispatched).

- Websites can be used to compare the prices of different suppliers before deciding which one to purchase.

- Deliveries can be tracked and traced via the websites of logistical companies.

- Computer programs (e.g. a database or spreadsheet) can be used to store inventory levels.

- EPOS (see page 71) can provide automatic updates on inventory and sales levels.

- Computer-aided design (CAD) and augmented reality (AR) can be used in the research and design stage of a new product before it is manufactured.

- Computer-aided manufacture (CAM) involves using computer-controlled equipment and robots in the manufacturing of a product (e.g. automation).

- 3D printing can be used to develop a prototype of a product before it is mass produced.

- Barcodes or QR codes can be used to keep track of inventory as it moves from warehouse to customer.

> ⚠ **Watch point**
>
> Be able to give examples of when technology could be used in operations.

Class activity

The Amazon Fulfillment Centre in Dunfermline allows classes to visit. A visit will allow you to see how Amazon manages its inventory, uses technology and gets its products to the customer quickly. You could also find out about the range of facilities and services it offers its staff.

Ask your teacher to arrange a visit if they can. If you can't visit, do some research into the points above instead.

Skills

- Applying

Questions

1. Describe the following methods of maintaining quality:
   - quality management
   - benchmarking
   - mystery shopping
   - quality symbol

2. Justify the use of each method given in Q1.
3. Describe the features of fair trade.
4. Describe methods that a business could adopt to protect the environment.
5. Describe a cost and a benefit of each method given in Q4.
6. Compare CAD and CAM.
7. Describe ways technology could be used in the inventory management process.

Key questions

1. Describe the features of an inventory management control system.
2. Outline the purposes of an inventory management control system.
3. Explain methods that can be used to ensure quality.
4. Explain the benefits and costs of different production methods used by large organisations.
5. Describe how technology can be used in the operations function.

Summary

This chapter provided you with an overview of how inventory can be managed, different methods of production and ways businesses can ensure quality. Environmental and ethical issues were explored, as was the role of technology in operations.

The main topics in this chapter were:

- Inventory management
- Methods of production
- Quality
- Ethical and environmental
- Technology in operations

By successfully answering the key questions, you will show that you have grasped the main topics covered in this chapter.

4 END OF CHAPTER MATERIAL

Sample exam question

Make sure you read each exam question carefully as every word is there for a reason. It is good practice to break each question down into parts before you answer it so that you know what is required.

For example:

Discuss methods of ensuring quality. (6 marks)

The command word – NB discuss means to make a number of points on a topic.

Plural – so you must give at least two methods.

Sample answer

An organisation can ensure quality in a number of different ways. It could use quality assurance, which is when products are checked at different stages of production **(1 mark)**. This allows any problems to be identified as early as possible to reduce the possible number of products that might go to waste **(1 mark)**. It could also use quality control, which is when a check takes place at the end of production **(1 mark)**. Benchmarking is another method, which is when the organisation attempts to produce a product that matches, or exceeds, the standard of the market-leading product **(1 mark)**. Finally, quality circles could be used, where members of the organisation get together to discuss quality issues **(1 mark)**. This can be motivating to those involved as they are involved in finding solutions to quality problems **(1 mark)**.

⚠ Watch point

When a specific number of examples is not asked for in an exam question, look carefully to see if the question is written in singular or plural form. Then, look carefully at the number of marks to help you decide how many points you need to make. Remember, one example can gain more than 1 mark if you write enough correct points!

Examiner's comments

The candidate discussed four methods of ensuring quality (quality assurance, quality control, benchmarking and quality circles). They correctly used knowledge of quality assurance and quality control from National 5 to help them answer the question. Even though they only discussed four methods, they were able to gain more marks because they developed their answer. No marks would be awarded for simply naming the method of ensuring quality in this question. **(6/6 marks)**

More sample exam questions

- Compare job and batch production. (6 marks)
- Compare centralised and decentralised methods of storage. (6 marks)
- Explain methods of ensuring quality. (6 marks)
- Describe the benefits of using benchmarking. (3 marks)
- Compare labour and capital intensive production. (3 marks)
- Describe the features of an inventory control system. (6 marks)
- Explain the benefits and costs of just in time. (6 marks)
- Define the terms 'automation' and 'mechanisation'. (2 marks)
- Suggest advantages of using robots in the production process. (3 marks)
- Describe ways technology could be used to support the operations function. (4 marks)
- Discuss the features of a fair trade product. (4 marks)
- Describe ways a business could be ethical in its operations. (6 marks)
- Explain the consequences of a business not operating ethically. (3 marks)

Check your progress

	HELP NEEDED	GETTING THERE	CONFIDENT
Inventory management	◯	◯	◯
Methods of production	◯	◯	◯
Centralised and decentralised storage	◯	◯	◯
Labour and capital intensive production	◯	◯	◯
Methods of quality	◯	◯	◯
Ethical and environmental	◯	◯	◯
Technology in operations	◯	◯	◯

5 Management of People

From National 5 you should already be able to:

- Describe stages of the recruitment process.
- Describe methods and types of training and outline their costs and benefits.
- Examine methods of motivating staff and outline their costs and benefits.
- Outline current employment legislation.

What you will learn about in this chapter:

- Workforce planning.
- Recruitment and selection.
- Training and development.
- Motivation and leadership.
- Employee relations.
- Legislation.
- Technology in human resources.

Workforce planning

⚠ **Watch point**

Look out for examples of how technology is used in various ways in human resources throughout this chapter.

Workforce or human resource planning enables an organisation to ensure that they have the correct employees in place at the right time to meet the needs of the organisation. Workforce planning involves analysing what needs to be done in an organisation and attempting to match suitably qualified and skilled staff to achieve the organisation's objectives.

It involves monitoring changes and trends in the labour market to establish changes in employment patterns. It is essential to be able to identify and estimate which employees will be required in the future and whether changes to existing staff levels, contracts and working practices need to be made. Workforce planning also involves considering the skills that will be required to carry out future job roles and then developing the appropriate training programmes to meet these requirements.

 Revision activity

Download and complete the revision sheet from the Leckie & Leckie website. This looks at the different stages of the recruitment process.

Recruitment

At National 5, the stages of the recruitment process were explored. At Higher, we need to look at internal and external recruitment.

Job vacancies can be advertised internally or externally, and therefore are available to internal candidates only or to internal and external candidates.

Internal recruitment

Internal recruitment is when the job vacancy is only advertised within the organisation and therefore only people already working for the organisation can apply for it. The vacancy might be circulated via e-mail, advertised on an intranet site or an advert put on the notice board.

Benefits	Costs
• Job vacancy can be filled quickly. • Employees are already known by the organisation and, if chosen, will have been so because they have demonstrated they have the ability to do the job. • Employees feel more valued and can become more motivated and productive if given the chance of promotion. • Money can be saved on advertising a job, recruiting, selecting and training, thereby increasing profitability. • Existing employees are already familiar with the policies, procedures and culture within the organisation and therefore do not need to be given guidance on this.	• The opportunity to gain new ideas from a new employee is lost and this could mean that new solutions to problems are not discovered. • An existing employee with the correct skills or ability for the job might not be available, therefore the position may remain unfilled. • There might not be that many existing employees that can apply for the position. • If a candidate is recruited internally, this will consequently create another vacancy within the organisation. • Conflict amongst existing employees competing for the job might exist.

 Make the link

Job applicants may be kept up to date with the progress of their application via e-mail or by logging into the company's website if they applied online.

External recruitment

External recruitment is when the job vacancy is advertised both within and outwith the organisation and anyone can apply.

The job vacancy might be advertised in a number of places:

- in the recruitment section of appropriate newspapers or magazines

- on recruitment websites such as s1jobs.com

- in a Jobcentre or via specialist recruitment agencies

- on websites designed for networking and professional purposes (e.g. LinkedIn)

- on the website of the organisation.

Individual activity

Create a LinkedIn profile to show your skills, achievements and qualifications to date. Add your classmates as contacts so that you can network with them once you finish your education!

Skills

- Employability
- Applying

External recruitment benefits and costs

Benefits	Costs
• People with new ideas can be brought into the organisation and can help enhance the effectiveness of the organisation. • External recruitment may attract large quantities of applicants so that the organisation has a range of people to choose from (however, this could be a disadvantage as it will be more time consuming to look at large quantities of applications). • Job vacancies can be filled quickly using the help of recruitment agencies. • Conflict that may arise between competing employees within an organisation if only internal recruitment is used may be avoided. • Specialist newspapers, magazines and agencies can be used to find appropriate staff, e.g. for specialist posts.	• Existing employees who apply but do not get the job may feel unvalued and therefore lose the motivation to work hard. • It can be expensive to advertise a job externally, e.g. in a national newspaper, and is usually a more expensive form of recruitment compared to internal recruitment. • A more thorough selection process may be required, which can be expensive compared to internal recruitment. • There is always a chance that the wrong person is chosen as they are unknown to the organisation, despite employing a number of selection methods.

? Questions

1. Discuss the purpose of workforce planning.
2. Suggest benefits of workforce planning.
3. Compare internal and external recruitment.
4. Explain two benefits and two costs of internal recruitment.
5. Explain two benefits and two costs of external recruitment.
6. Suggest places where a job could be advertised externally.
7. Suggest how technology could be used in the recruitment process.

Selection

At National 5, some methods of selection such as application forms, CVs and references were explored. At Higher, we need to look at some other selection methods in more detail.

Interviews

Interviews are a common selection method. They allow the organisation to meet applicants, ask them questions and find out whether or not they are suitable for the job vacancy. They also allow the applicant to ask questions to see whether or not the vacancy is for them. Sometimes applicants might be asked to do a short presentation in the interview, using presentation software.

One-to-one interviews

One interviewer interviews all of the short-listed applicants and then makes a decision on who to select. This type of interview is not uncommon, but has a distinct disadvantage in that the interviewer may not like a particular person for some reason (e.g. personality) and this could lead to the wrong person being given the job. However, it is cheaper than successive or panel interviews.

Successive interviews

Several interviewers interview each applicant separately. Unfortunately, it means that the applicant has a number of interviews to attend. However, it does have the advantage over one-to-one interviews in that it avoids interviewer bias.

Panel interviews

A panel interview involves one applicant being interviewed by several people at one time. Each person on the interview panel asks a number of questions and each member has a final say in who is selected. Each member of the interview panel will compare their notes on each candidate before making a final decision. Someone will be appointed to chair the interview panel and there would normally be a mixture of genders for equality purposes.

> ### ☀: Make the link
>
> Interviews do not need to take place face-to-face. Interviews could take place electronically via, for example, Skype or videoconferencing.

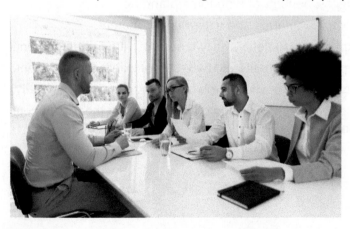

Testing

A variety of tests can be carried out to help in the selection process. Each test will assess a different aspect of the applicant's abilities or skills and can confirm what the applicant has written on their application form or CV. Tests can be expensive to carry out and are time consuming. They need to be carried out carefully because, just like exams, people can perform worse than expected because of the pressure and stress imposed on them.

Make the link

Tests can often be carried out online and the results made available to an organisation instantly.

Psychometric/ psychological tests	In these tests, applicants are asked questions that assess their personality. The tests can be used to find out what type of person they are and whether they suit the requirements of the job. Unlike some other types of tests, there is no correct answer and applicants should give truthful answers so that an accurate picture of their personality can be built up. However, this does not always happen and applicants might select the answer that they think the organisation wants to hear. This type of test can establish whether or not someone would fit into a particular culture (e.g. a sales-driven environment) or one that is highly pressurised (e.g. air traffic control).
Aptitude tests	This test assesses the natural abilities of applicants on the skills required for a particular job they are applying for. Aptitude tests might assess literacy and numeracy skills. These skills might be important for jobs involving lots of reading and writing and/or working with numbers.
Intelligence tests	Also known as IQ tests, these assess the mental capability of the applicant. It might be that an applicant needs to be able to process lots of information that is being given quickly in a pressurised environment (e.g. emergency services) and this test would help to indicate whether or not they could do this.
Medical tests	A doctor or nurse examines each applicant for any medical issues or concerns that may impact upon their ability to perform the duties of the job. A questionnaire may also need to be completed. Some occupations (e.g. pilots) have strict medical conditions that need to be met.
Attainment tests	An attainment test allows an applicant to demonstrate that they have a specific skill, for example in ICT. A typing test, for example, might be given to a potential administrative assistant to see how many words they can type per minute.

Paired activity

Many websites offer you the opportunity to carry out different types of tests. Search the internet for different types of tests. Try doing some of them to see how you get on!

Skills

• Applying

Group activity

In small groups, choose one of the following jobs:

- Market researcher
- Quality supervisor
- Administrative assistant
- Finance manager

Create a list of interview questions that might be asked at the interview for your chosen job. For each question, give reasons why that question is being asked and what answer you would expect to obtain from it.

Think about any tests that might be carried out to help you make a decision on who should get the job. Justify why each test has been chosen.

Make a list of any other selection methods that you would use for the job with reasons why they have been chosen.

Skills

- Applying
- Analysing & evaluating

Assessment centres

Assessment centres allow an organisation to see a large number of applicants undertaking a variety of tasks in different situations and realistic work-related scenarios. They quite often take place over a couple of days. Applicants may have to take part in team building activities, role play tasks and deliver presentations. Tests may also need to be undertaken. At all points during the assessment centre, the organisation will be watching the applicant carefully and making a note of their communication, leadership, team work and problem solving skills.

 Make the link

Presentation software could be used to create and deliver a presentation.

Assessment centres are expensive to carry out as they require significant preparation beforehand and the organisation needs to have the necessary facilities to conduct it. Several members of staff also need to be available to supervise and conduct the assessment centre. As several members of the organisation are involved, it reduces the possibility of interviewer bias.

? Questions

1. Define the following terms:
   - CV
   - application form
   - reference.
2. Describe the purpose of a job interview.
3. Explain two benefits and two costs of an interview.
4. Describe different types of interviews.
5. Justify the use of tests in the selection process.
6. Describe the purpose of four types of tests.
7. Describe the purpose of an assessment centre.
8. Discuss the benefits and costs of an assessment centre.

Training and development

At National 5, we looked at three types of training: induction, on-the-job and off-the-job. You should make sure you go back and revise these. At Higher, we need to explore different methods of staff development, training schemes and work-based qualifications.

Continuing professional development

Organisations need to provide their staff with opportunities to develop as individuals and as employees. Training allows people to carry out their jobs better and gives them the opportunity to learn new skills. Staff development is an important part of being able to provide a high-quality product or service.

☀ Revision activity

Download and complete the revision sheet from the Leckie & Leckie website. This looks at the different types of training.

⚠ Watch point

Many work-based training schemes are credit rated and levelled through the Scottish Credit and Qualifications Framework (SCQF).

Make the link

Databases can record employee information, including records of their CPD.

Most organisations accept that training should not be provided on a one-off basis, but instead opportunities for learning should be continually provided. Providing opportunities for development is important in being able to achieve the organisation's objectives in a changing business environment. The Scottish Government has a life-long learning agenda and has invested significant sums of money into providing opportunities for people of all ages to learn new skills and gain qualifications.

A record of all continuing professional development (CPD) that an employee undertakes is normally kept and quite often when an employee is requesting training, they need to demonstrate how this matches what the organisation is trying to achieve. Evaluation after CPD is also carried out so that it can be discussed at the annual appraisal interview between the employee and their line manager.

Virtual learning environment (VLE)

Many organisations now offer employees the opportunity to participate in CPD through virtual learning facilities. This is usually a specific password-protected website that people can log into to access training materials.

Benefits	Costs
• Can be accessed at any time of the day in any location. • Large numbers of people can access it. • Can be updated easily with notes, tasks, videos and other materials. • Saves on printing costs and is more environmentally friendly than providing hard copies of training materials. • Interaction between users can take place through discussion forums and live chat facilities.	• People need to be self-disciplined to access the facility and carry out the activities. • People may prefer face-to-face contact rather than virtual learning; it might not suit their own learning style. • Might be expensive to employ a specialist to set up and maintain a virtual learning facility.

Training schemes and work-based qualifications

Many organisations offer their employees the opportunity to gain work-based qualifications. Sometimes these qualifications may be assessed in-house by a trained assessor or may involve someone from a local college or training provider visiting the organisation to carry out the assessment. In Scotland, work-based qualifications include Scottish Vocational Qualifications (SVQs) and are available at different SCQF levels.

Benefits	Costs
• A recognised qualification (sometimes SCQF credit rated) can be obtained. • Training can take place on-the-job and tailored to the organisation's specific needs. • Promotion opportunities might be greater for employees. • Records of training time can be kept by the employee, therefore contributing towards any minimum contractual CPD requirements.	• Can be time consuming to carry out alongside existing work. • Can be expensive to pay for external trainers/bodies to provide and/or assess work-based qualifications. • Once trained or awarded a work-based qualification, employees might seek employment opportunities elsewhere. • Apprentices are not guaranteed a permanent (open-ended) contract once the apprenticeship is complete.

Glasgow Kelvin College

 Individual activity

Visit the website of your local college to find out what work-based qualifications they have to offer.

 Skills

• Applying

In some industries (e.g. plumbing, joinery), people learn their trade by carrying out an apprenticeship. An apprenticeship is when someone learns on the job and may attend a local college for part of the work to gain a recognised qualification. Apprenticeships can take a number of years to complete. There are currently 3 types of apprenticeship: modern apprenticeship, foundation apprenticeship and graduate apprenticeship and further details can be obtained from the Skills Development Scotland website.

 Individual activity

Visit the Skills Development Scotland apprenticeship web pages. Find out:

• The difference between each type of apprenticeship (modern, foundation and graduate).
• The benefits of undertaking an apprenticeship.
• What apprenticeship opportunities are available in your area.

 Skills

• Applying
• Analysing & evaluating

❓ Questions

1. Compare on-the-job and off-the-job training.
2. Describe the purpose of induction training.
3. Define the term 'CPD'.
4. Discuss the benefits and costs of CPD.
5. Define the term 'VLE'.
6. Explain the environmental benefits of having a VLE compared to paper-based methods.
7. Suggest other benefits and costs of a VLE.
8. Describe the purpose of an SVQ.
9. Explain the benefits and costs of having a work-based qualifications scheme.
10. Define the term apprenticeship.

⚠ **Watch point**

Make sure you can suggest ways of motivating staff and be able to give reasons why those methods motivate staff.

Motivation and leadership

At National 5, we explored different financial and non-financial incentives that can be used to motivate employees. We will look at some of these further at Higher and also at different theories of motivation and leadership that organisations could employ.

💡 **Revision activity**

Download and complete the revision sheet from the Leckie & Leckie website. This looks at the methods of motivating staff and working practices.

Motivation strategy	Benefits of strategy
Providing fair pay for the work that employees do	Employees will work harder if they think they are being rewarded fairly for their work. If they don't think their work is being rewarded fairly, this will decrease their productivity.
Empowering employees with responsibility for carrying out a particular task or duty	Some people are motivated by being given extra responsibility as it gives them the opportunity to demonstrate what they are capable of doing. Some people are not motivated by carrying out routine, repetitive tasks.
Avoid the use of temporary contracts if possible	People who are on temporary contracts have no job security as they are only employed for a short period of time. Offering permanent (or open-ended) contracts gives people the knowledge that their position is secure.
Provide opportunities for continuing professional development	People will feel valued by the fact that they are being given the opportunity to learn and gain work-related qualifications. This will encourage them to work harder and will also allow them to carry out their job to a better standard.
Offer incentives (e.g. bonuses) for achieving targets	Incentives such as bonuses can be used to encourage people to work harder and achieve more. Salespeople are often paid commission or bonuses to encourage them to sell as much as they can. People working in a factory might be paid piece rate to encourage them to produce as many units as possible.
Having an open door policy	An open door policy will encourage employees to talk to their managers about different issues. This type of policy may allow issues to be resolved before they become out of control.
Empower employees	Empowerment gives employees the authority to make decisions without having to consult their manager. This can motivate people as they are seen to be trusted to make decisions by the organisation.

Motivation theories

Theories of motivation can be used to help understand what motivates people. They can be applied in an organisation to motivate employees. Different theorists have different ideas about what motivates people at work.

Maslow's hierarchy of needs

Maslow suggested that there are five levels of human needs that can be satisfied. Each level must be satisfied before someone can progress to the next level, starting at the bottom of the pyramid. If something is not satisfied at one level, they cannot progress to the next. When needs at one level are met, they are no longer motivating.

 Group discussion

Starting with physiological needs, discuss what a business could do to try and satisfy each level of Maslow's hierarchy of needs for its employees.

 Skills

- Applying

 Watch point

You should be able to discuss each level of Maslow's hierarchy and be able to give specific examples of each level in relation to the management of people.

Realising potential and purpose. Being able to be creative and spontaneous. At work, this might be achieved through more responsibility and using creativity to solve problems. — Self-actualisation

Achieving respect from others and recognised as an individual. At work, this could involve being promoted, leading a project or working group, praise or opportunities for leadership training. — Self-esteem

Belonging to a group, e.g. friends and family. At work, this would include good working relationships and a sense of belonging to the organisation. — Love and belonging

Safety needs include health and social stability. In relation to work, job security and good working conditions, e.g. safety equipment and paying the national living wage. — Safety and security

Basic needs such as food, water, air and shelter. Pay for work is also a basic need. — Physiological needs

Leadership theories

Leaders in an organisation attempt to influence people to encourage them to work towards achieving organisational goals. A leader might be a manager, but might not.

McGregor X and Y

McGregor suggested that there were two different types of managers: Theory X and Theory Y. Each type of manager makes different assumptions about their employees and this influences how the leader behaves.

Theory X	Theory Y
The Theory X leader believes that employees do not like work and try to avoid it. It is assumed that employees have no drive or ambition and are not interested in being given responsibility or empowerment. As a result, the leader has to exercise tight control over what is going on and make all the decisions.	The Theory Y leader believes that work provides people with satisfaction and a sense of achievement. Employees are happy to work hard towards achieving the goals of the organisation. As a result, the leader provides opportunities for development and empowerment. The leader delegates responsibility to employees where they can.

Iowa leadership studies

Lewin, Lippit and White carried out a study at the University of Iowa. They believe that there are three styles of leaders:

Autocratic	Authority and power rests with the leader. Decisions are made by the leader and are implemented using fear of punishment. Communication tends to be one directional and there is no opportunity for employee involvement, empowerment or delegation.
Democratic	The democratic or participate leader believes in consultation and communication with their employees. The leader believes that people are important and all have a valuable contribution to make towards decision-making. This type of leadership is often seen as motivating and can improve decision-making, as many people are involved in the process. However, it can mean that decision-making takes longer.
Laissez-faire	The laissez-faire leader does not exercise any control over their employees and people are really left to get on with things themselves. Support and guidance are only provided by the leader when requested. There is little direction given to the group, which can lead to limited achievement of organisational goals.

In an organisation, there might be a range of people who each have a different leadership style. In some organisations, some styles are more appropriate than others.

Group activity

Make a list of different leaders from the news or that you know of. What style of leader are they? Give examples to justify your choice.

Skills

- Applying
- Analysing & evaluating

? Questions

1. Describe and justify three ways of motivating staff.
2. Describe the purpose of motivation theories.
3. Discuss the use of Maslow's hierarchy of needs.
4. Compare a Theory X manager and a Theory Y manager.
5. Describe three different types of leaders according to Lewin, Lippit and White.
6. Suggest the benefits and costs of different types of leaders given in Q5.

Employee relations

Having motivated employees is a key factor to success in any organisation. Employees lie at the heart of the organisation and are crucial in helping it to achieve its aims. The relationship between employee and employer is important. Good employee relations can impact on an organisation in a number of ways:

- Staff turnover (the number of people leaving the organisation) will decrease, which will reduce costs associated with recruitment, selection, training and development.

- The number of days staff are absent will reduce, which means productivity will be higher and more customer needs can be satisfied.

- Employees will be more motivated and happier at work, which will result in customers receiving a better standard of service that will encourage them to return and also to provide positive feedback about the organisation.

- Employees will be more willing to accept and adapt to any changes in the organisation as a result of the changing business environment; this will make implementing decisions easier as staff are not resistant to them.

 ⚠ Watch point

Make sure you can explain how good employee relations can impact an organisation.

Good employee relations can be formed in a number of ways. Providing financial and non-financial incentives, such as those discussed when we looked at motivation, can be useful, but there are other ways to foster a good relationship.

Trade unions	Trade unions represent the views of employees on different employment-related matters. This might include pay, conditions, dismissal and any grievances. Employees have the option of joining a trade union when they begin a job but do not have to do so. There is usually an annual fee payable. Trade unions act on behalf of their members and have a much larger voice, more experience and are in a more powerful position to negotiate than individual employees on their own. (This is known as collective bargaining.)
Works councils	A works council is formed with representatives from across the organisation. It has the ability to access various types of information that relate to the organisation and it has the authority to take part in making decisions, alongside management, that relate to the workforce. Representatives from the works council might sit on various committees within the organisation.
Quality circles	See page 110 for more information on quality circles.
Worker directors	A worker who represents employees on management boards and committees. They represent the views of the employees who work for the organisation. This allows employees via the worker director to have an input on decision-making and matters impacting upon the company and them. It also allows the organisation to hear the opinions of those 'on the ground' and who have knowledge of day-to-day activities and routines.
Consultative committees	Usually a short-term committee set up to consult on a particular issue or decision, e.g. to merge or to close specific stores. It allows people to express their views to the committee before a final decision is then made by the organisation.

Contemporary working practices

We looked at the different working practices covered at National 5. At Higher, we need to think about why there has been a change in working practices over the past several years.

- There has been an increase in employment opportunities in the tertiary and quaternary sectors at the same time as a decrease in the primary and secondary sectors (see pages 8–9).

- More people are becoming employed on part-time and temporary contracts compared to full-time or permanent ones to meet the needs of organisations that have to operate in a changing business and economic environment.

- More women are now in employment in both full-time and part-time jobs and there has also been an increase in the number of women who have management positions.

- Developments in technology have allowed more people to work out of the office either as homeworkers or teleworkers.

- The Government has encouraged people to become enterprising and as a result people are opting to become self-employed.

- There has been an increase in the number of small businesses opening up because of the increase in people starting their own business.

- There has been an increase in the number of people undertaking short-term contracts because of growth in the 'gig economy'.

> **GO! Group activity**
>
> Make a list of different pieces of technology that could be used by people working outwith the office environment. Justify the use of each piece of technology.
>
> **Y Skills**
>
> - Applying
> - Analysing & evaluating

Industrial action

Employees who are unhappy with their working conditions or terms of employment, and where discussions have not reached an agreement, have the option of undertaking industrial action. This would only be classed as 'official' when a trade union has agreed that this should take place. Different forms of industrial action were explored at National 5.

It is important to remember that industrial action does not always resolve the dispute between employee and employer. Sometimes the employer might threaten to make employees redundant if they refuse to accept the terms or conditions given to them.

💡 Revision activity

Download and complete the revision sheet from the Leckie & Leckie website. This looks at different forms of industrial action.

GO! Paired or group activity

Find an example in the news of industrial action that has taken place recently. Find out:

- What form of industrial action took place and why.
- The consequences of the industrial action on different stakeholders.
- What action was taken to resolve the dispute and how successful it was.

Be prepared to present your findings to the rest of your class.

🌳 Skills

- Applying
- Analysing & evaluating

Redundancy

Redundancy is when an employee or a number of employees are paid off because their job is no longer required or no longer exists. It is not the same as 'firing' someone. It can happen when the organisation can no longer afford to pay the number of employees it has or when a demand for the organisation's product has decreased. By law, organisations have a strict procedure to follow when making staff redundant and must usually make redundancy payments to those people being laid off.

Employees who are not being made redundant may worry about the safety of their own jobs and the quality of their work can suffer. They may be required to undertake additional tasks or duties as a result of fewer people working for the organisation. This can consequently increase their own workload and may require them to be re-trained to carry out new tasks.

Grievances

A grievance is when an employee has a complaint to make to their employer regarding a work-related issue. They may be unhappy about something they have been asked to do or because of the way they feel they have been treated. Organisations will have in place a grievance procedure that will identify the steps an employee needs to follow when making a grievance. As a last resort, an employee can take their grievance to Acas (Advisory, Conciliation and Arbitration Service) or to an industrial tribunal. Acas is an organisation that specialises in resolving disputes and disagreements between employees and their employers.

GO! Individual activity

Visit the Acas website at www.acas.org.uk to find out more about what they do.

Skills

• Applying

Appraisals

An appraisal is normally an annual formal meeting between an employee and employer to discuss the employee's work performance (their strengths and development needs) – this is known as a **one-to-one appraisal**. It is a two-way process as the employee will receive feedback from their employer, but the employee is also expected to think about and evaluate their own performance. An appraisal system aims to ensure employees are working to the best possible standard with the goal of achieving the organisation's aims. An appraisal can be motivating or demotivating for an employee depending on how it is carried out and whether or not it is seen as a positive or negative experience. At an appraisal, the following questions might be discussed:

- What is going well?

- What is not going so well?

- What could be done better?

- What action could be taken to make things better?

A written record of the appraisal meeting will be kept and where an employee has development needs, the employee would normally be given the opportunity to undertake CPD or training as appropriate.

Benefits	Costs
• Employees who have the potential for promotion can be identified. • Feedback is given to the employee by their line manager to improve their work; praise can be given for work done well. • Can be a motivating experience if the appraisal is positive. • Opportunities for CPD and training can be identified. • Targets for future performance can be discussed and agreed.	• Some employees might see the appraisal as a 'tick-box' exercise and not take it seriously or commit to it. • Can be a demotivating experience if the appraisal is negative. • It is a time-consuming process to carry out; other activities are not being completed when an appraisal meeting is taking place. • An employee might have too many development needs, which could result in additional stress for them and an increased workload.

Other appraisal systems include:

- **Peer-to-peer appraisal** – when a colleague at the same level of the hierarchy conducts the appraisal. The colleague provides feedback to the employee on their work and suggestions on things to improve. Supervisors, team leaders or managers (depending on the structure of the organisation) do not contribute to the appraisal of the individual.

- **360 degree appraisal** – feedback from a number of sources (e.g. colleagues, subordinates, supervisors) is used to assess the employee's work performance. The employee also self-evaluates themselves to inform the appraisal. Each person involved in the process is normally asked the same questions and thus allows for a range of views to be obtained.

- **Informal appraisal** – no formal structure is followed, instead a chat between an employee and employer takes place; the employee might receive feedback on how to do something better or they might be praised for doing a job well.

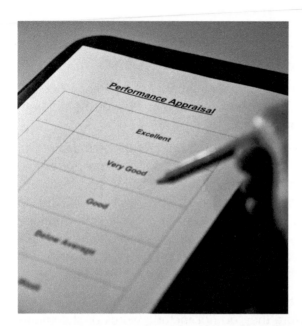

? Questions

1. Explain three benefits of having good employee relations.
2. Explain three consequences of having poor employee relations.
3. Define the term 'trade union'.
4. Define the term 'works council'.
5. Suggest reasons why a range of working practices are now offered by organisations.
6. Describe two benefits and two costs of flexible working practices.
7. Describe each of the following working practices:
   - hot-desking
   - teleworking
   - job share
   - annualised hours
   - flexitime.
8. Describe five forms of industrial action.
9. Define the term 'redundancy'.
10. Define the term 'grievance'.
11. Outline the consequences of a grievance for an organisation.
12. Describe the purpose of Acas.
13. Explain two benefits and two costs of an appraisal system.
14. Describe two types of appraisal.

Make the link

At National 5, we also looked at health and safety legislation.

⚠ **Watch point**

Be able to give examples of what an employer must do to comply with pieces of legislation. It is not enough at Higher to simply know what the legislation is – the impact of it is important.

Legislation

The Equality Act 2010

The Equality Act brings together a number of different aspects of equality under one piece of legislation. Previously, different pieces of legislation existed.

The Act states that people must not be discriminated against on the basis of 'protected characteristics'. These protected characteristics are race, gender, sexual orientation, age, disability, religion, pregnancy and maternity. This applies not just to employees of a business, but also to the people who purchase goods and services. Managers of a business need to be aware of this legislation because they will need to take certain actions to ensure the business remains within the law. For example:

- When advertisements for jobs are being created, managers need to ensure they do not include words or statements about the person they are looking for that might be seen to break the law, e.g. they could not say 'a young person is required' as this would indicate age discrimination.

- Barriers to physically accessing the business will need to be considered and, where possible, action taken to make the business more accessible (e.g. by installing lifts or ramps to enable people with a disability to access the business).

- If an employee or customer feels that they are being discriminated against on the basis of one or more of the protected characteristics, the organisation has a duty to investigate this and take action where necessary.

- Policies may need to be created to ensure that all employees of the business are aware of the legislation and what they need to do to comply with it.

Non-compliance with the Act may result in prosecution.

Employment Rights Act 1996

This Act states the legal rights of employees in the workplace. It states that:

- Employees are entitled to receive a written statement of the terms and conditions of employment; this means that an employer will need to produce this and provide their employees with a copy of it.

- Employees have the right to an itemised pay slip; employers will need to have a record keeping system in place to record such pay information and to produce this for each employee when they are being paid.

- Employees have the right not to be unfairly dismissed; employers will need to have a policy in place covering dismissal from the workplace that clearly sets out the process to be followed if a disciplinary or dismissal issue became apparent.

- Employees are entitled to redundancy provisions if they were to be made redundant.

National Minimum Wage Regulations

These set out the lowest amount of pay a person can receive per hour. The current minimum wage (as of October 2019) is:

Age	Rate
25 and over	£8.21 per hour
21 to 24	£7.70 per hour
18 to 20	£6.15 per hour
Under 18	£4.35 per hour
Apprentice	£3.90 per hour

Employers need to make sure they have the funds in place to be able to pay their employees the required minimum wage. This might mean having to budget carefully to ensure they can make the required payments on time.

Some organisations may decide to pay the **National Living Wage**, which is higher than the minimum wage (currently £9.30 per hour). Organisations who pay the National Living Wage, compared to the minimum wage, are able to highlight this to prospective staff and other stakeholders.

> **GO! Individual activity**
>
> Find examples throughout this chapter for when technology can be used in human resources.
> Can you think of any others to add to the list?
>
> **Skills**
>
> - Applying

> ★ **Key questions**
>
> 1. Describe approaches that could be used to effectively manage human resources.
> 2. Describe approaches that could be used to effectively motivate staff.
> 3. Explain how employee effectiveness can impact upon the success of a large organisation.
> 4. Describe the impact of current employment legislation.

Summary

This chapter provided you with an overview of the methods that can be employed to ensure that there are sufficient and suitably qualified human resources available in an organisation. It also explored the importance and consequences of employee relations and the impact of employment legislation on an organisation. Examples of how technology can be used in managing human resources were explored throughout.

The main topics in this chapter were:

- Workforce planning
- Recruitment and selection
- Training and development
- Motivation and leadership
- Employee relations
- Legislation
- Technology in human resources

By successfully answering the key questions, you will show that you have grasped the main topics covered in this chapter.

5 END OF CHAPTER MATERIAL

Sample exam question

Make sure you read each exam question carefully as every word is there for a reason. It is good practice to break each question down into parts before you answer it so that you know what is required.

For example:

Discuss the role of technology in human resources. (6 marks)

> The command word – NB discuss means to make a number of points on a topic.

> The question is specifically about human resources, not how technology could be used in other functions.

Sample answer

A company's website could be set up to allow job applicants to apply online for a job and upload their CV **(1 mark)**. E-mail could then be used by the organisation to invite job applicants to an interview **(1 mark)**. At the job interview, applicants might be asked to make a presentation, using presentation software, about their suitability for a job **(1 mark)**. They may also have to answer different questions about their personality (a personality test) on a computer **(1 mark)**. Once the organisation has employed someone, their personal information and records could be stored on a database **(1 mark)**. The organisation might carry out staff training via their VLE **(1 mark)**.

> ⚠ **Watch point**
>
> Be careful when answering a question on technology. It will usually be specific to a function, e.g. marketing, human resources, operations or finance. Your answer must clearly link the technology to the function.

Examiner's comments

The candidate discussed six different pieces of technology and made specific reference to how each piece would be used in human resources. **(6/6 marks)**

More sample exam questions

- Compare internal and external recruitment. (4 marks)
- Describe and justify different types of interview. (6 marks)
- Explain the benefits of using an assessment centre. (3 marks)
- Describe and justify methods that can be used to motivate staff. (6 marks)
- Describe different types of appraisal systems. (6 marks)
- Discuss how an organisation could achieve an employee's basic and safety/security needs. (4 marks)
- Explain the benefits of good employee relations. (6 marks)
- Describe actions that need to be taken to comply with two pieces of employment legislation. (6 marks)
- Explain the benefits and costs of using technology in human resources. (6 marks)

Check your progress

	NEED HELP	GETTING THERE	CONFIDENT
Workforce planning	◯	◯	◯
Recruitment and selection	◯	◯	◯
Training and development	◯	◯	◯
Motivation and leadership	◯	◯	◯
Employee relations	◯	◯	◯
Legislation	◯	◯	◯
Technology in human resources	◯	◯	◯

6 Management of Finance

From National 5 you should already be able to:

- Describe sources of finance and outline their costs and benefits.
- Interpret a break-even chart.
- Interpret a cash budget to identify cash flow issues and outline appropriate solutions.
- Prepare a simple income statement from data provided.

What you will learn about in this chapter:

- The role of finance.
- Sources of finance.
- Cash budgeting.
- Financial statements.
- Ratios.
- Technology in finance.

The role of finance

At National 5 we explored the role of finance and looked at some of the sources of finance for a small-to-medium-sized business. At Higher, we also need to look at the sources of finance available to larger organisations such as plcs and multinationals.

The role of the finance department in a larger organisation is:

To control costs and expenses
Costs and expenses must be controlled to avoid financial problems and the need to borrow money to cover these costs. Where necessary, management might have to take action to reduce costs and the amount of money going out of the organisation. Costs and expenses can be recorded in a spreadsheet package and graphs produced to show trends over a period of time.

To monitor cash flow going in and out of the business
Money coming into the organisation and going out of the organisation needs to be monitored. There needs to be enough 'cash' available to be able to pay suppliers, trade payables and employee wages. Making profit and having a good cash flow are two different things.

To forecast what might happen in the future

Preparing budgets and looking at past financial statements can help to identify trends and to see what might happen in the future. Action can be taken if necessary to avoid financial problems.

To monitor performance

Financial information can be used to compare one year against a previous year to see if performance has improved. This is useful to see if action taken in the past has worked and, where necessary, to take action in the future. Ratio analysis (see page 158) can be used to help monitor performance.

To provide information for decision-making

We already know that managers make lots of decisions. Financial information plays a crucial role in decision-making and will often influence which course of action is taken. PowerPoint presentations can be used to display financial information at meetings (which could also be held via Skype or by videoconferencing without the need to travel).

Financial information

Different pieces of financial information can be used by different stakeholders.

Make the link

Technology can be used in a variety of ways in the Finance department. Make a list of the different ways technology can be used in finance as you read this chapter.

Make the link

Employee pay is usually paid directly into an employee's bank account using BACS (banking automated clearing services) on a specific date, e.g. each month.

Make the link

Individuals and businesses can check their online tax account at anytime using the HMRC website.

Make the link

Suppliers might send their invoices for payment by e-mail.

Stakeholder	Why they use it
Employees	• To check to see whether or not they are being paid fairly (e.g. is the business making large profits but not agreeing to a pay increase?). • To understand why certain decisions are being made (e.g. redundancies).
Inland Revenue (HMRC)	• To check that the correct amount of taxation is being paid.
Shareholders	• To help make a decision on how to vote at the annual general meeting (AGM) of shareholders. • To decide whether to purchase additional shares. • To decide if the organisation is paying a fair dividend based on the profit being made.
Suppliers and trade payables	• To decide whether or not to allow more credit. • To show how able a business is to pay off its debts.
Lenders (e.g. a bank)	• To determine whether or not a loan should be given. • To show how able a business is to pay off its debts.

There is no doubt that decisions and planning are based on a range of financial information, but there are limitations to this. Not all decisions can be based purely on how profitable the organisation is. Remember, most financial information is based on past events and transactions. In other words, it has already happened.

When judging how successful a business is, financial information cannot be used on its own. This is because it does not reveal anything about:

- How motivated staff are.

- The impact of external factors.

- Future plans or product developments.

- How successful the organisation has been in increasing market share.

- The stage at which each product is in its life cycle.

Sources of finance

In addition to the sources of finance covered at National 5, the following sources are also available to large organisations. The source of finance chosen by a company will depend on a variety of factors, e.g. purpose, interest rates/cost of finance and the payback terms and conditions.

Issuance of additional shares – limited companies could issue extra shares to new or existing shareholders. Plcs can sell their shares on the stock market.

Benefits	Costs
• Large amounts of capital can be obtained. • Shareholders benefit from limited liability. • The finance raised does not have to be paid back in the way loans do.	• The selling price of shares varies daily on the stock market. • Share issue can be expensive. • Only a certain number of shares can be issued.

Leasing – businesses could rent equipment or premises rather than buying these outright.

⚠ Watch point

Financial information is one indicator of how successful a business is, but it isn't the only one.

💡 Revision activity

Download and complete the revision sheet from the Leckie & Leckie website. This looks at the role of finance and sources of finance for smaller businesses.

Benefits	Costs
• Saves on having to purchase expensive equipment outright (helps to improve cash flow). • Equipment can be changed regularly and kept up to date.	• Leasing over a long period of time might prove more expensive compared to buying outright. • The leased item is not owned by the organisation and is therefore not an asset to them.

Venture capitalists (or business angels) – provide large loans to organisations that a bank or other lender may feel are too risky. They usually part-own the organisation in return for taking the risk.

Benefits	Costs
• Organisations who have a poor credit rating might be able to get finance from a venture capitalist instead of a bank, which sees them as too risky. • Large amounts of finance can be obtained.	• Not suitable for small sums of money or for short-term purposes. • Can be expensive. • Part ownership of the organisation may be a requirement of the loan.

Other sources of finance may include **debt factoring**, when debts are sold by the company to a debt factoring company who then tries to collect the money due. This saves the organisation time by not having to pursue the debt, but the debt might be sold to the debt factor for less than the original value. **Crowd funding** might be used by an organisation to gain public support for a particular project or initiative (although this is more commonly used in the public and third sector).

The stock market

The stock market is where sellers and buyers of shares in companies come together to sell and buy those shares. Public limited companies (see page 16) can sell their shares to raise finance. A person who buys shares in a company is known as a shareholder and is an owner of the company. Share prices for plcs can be obtained on the internet.

? Questions

1. Discuss the role of finance in an organisation.
2. Suggest the interests different stakeholders have in financial information.

3. Describe the factors not revealed in financial information.

4. Describe sources of finance available to larger organisations.

5. Explain the benefits and costs of each source given in Q4.

Cash budgeting

Cash is a crucial resource in any organisation. It is needed to pay bills, to purchase assets, to pay employees and to achieve different objectives. Most organisations have the aim of making a profit, but they also need cash on a day-to-day basis to operate. Making profit and having a healthy cash flow are two different things.

It is important that an organisation monitors its cash flow (or liquidity position) so that it can continue to meet its financial obligations and operate successfully. Failing to have a healthy cash flow can be caused by a number of factors:

- Having too much money tied up in inventory.

- Too much time being given to customers to pay their debt (a long credit period).

- Not enough money being generated from sales.

- Too short a credit period being offered by trade payables or suppliers.

- Too much drawings being taken out by the owners (or high dividends for a plc).

- Large sums of money being spent on capital items (e.g. machinery).

- Sudden increase in operating expenses.

Cash flow problems can be solved in a number of ways:

Method	Justification
Introduce a just-in-time (JIT) approach to inventory management (see page 101).	This will save money being tied up in inventory. By using a JIT system, inventory is only purchased when it is needed for an order.
Offer discounts to customers as an incentive to pay on time.	This will encourage customers to pay their bills more quickly and the cash received can be used to fund other activities.

Make the link

Online banking allows a company to check their cash balance at any time.

Make the link

Sources of finance (pages 145–146) can also be used to manage cash flow.

(continued)

Increase advertising and promotion activities.	Advertising can raise awareness of the organisation and its products. Different promotion activities (e.g. special offers) could be used to entice customers to buy. More purchases mean increased sales and cash flow and reduced inventory.
Sell non-current assets no longer required.	Selling assets that are no longer required will generate cash and, because they are not required by the organisation, this will not cause any disruption to the organisation's operations.

There are consequences of having poor cash flow:

- Suppliers may not receive payment for raw materials and therefore refuse to supply further materials, which could cause production to stop.

- Operating expenses (e.g. electricity) might not be paid and therefore these supplies could be cut off.

- Drawings taken by owners may have to be reduced or stopped and therefore they might be unwilling to invest more money into the company.

- Insufficient cash may result in employees not being paid on time, which could result in poor employee relations.

- Growth might be restricted because of the company's inability to purchase new stores, equipment or pay new employees.

Cash budgets

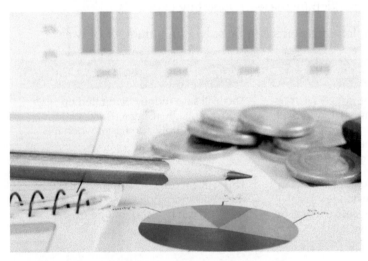

To help manage cash and ensure control over future cash flow, a cash budget can be prepared. This is a forecast of the money expected to be received **(receipts)** and the money expected to be paid out **(payments)** over a period of time.

The benefits of preparing a cash budget include:

- It shows whether the business will have a surplus (more cash expected to come in than will go out) or deficit (more cash expected to go out than will come in).

- It shows whether additional finance is required to ensure the business continues to operate effectively.

- It helps control expenses by highlighting periods when expenses could be high.

- It helps to make decisions, e.g. whether to launch into a new product area.

- It measures performance of departments (see below).

A cash budget could be used as a target for the organisation and different departments within the organisation to work towards. In a large organisation, each department may have its own budget and the authority for controlling (and spending) this budget would be delegated to the department's manager. Management could compare the actual spending of the department with the amount budgeted, to assess the department manager's skills in budgeting. It would be the responsibility of the department manager to ensure his/her department stays within budget and, where necessary, take action to ensure it does so.

Spreadsheet packages can be used to create cash budgets (and other financial statements). Calculations can be carried out by entering formulae. Formulae can be replicated across a spreadsheet to save time from manually entering them in. Graphs and charts can be created on a spreadsheet to compare trends in sales, expenses, profit and other financial information. More advanced functions, such as IF statements, can be used to see if a condition has been met (e.g. is receipts greater than payments in a cash budget).

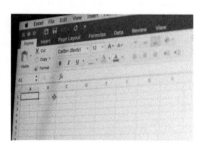

🔍 Case study

Real Fitness Plc has prepared a cash budget for January–March. It wants to make sure it has enough money coming in to cover different expenses.

Cash budget for January–March

	£ January	£ February	£ March
Opening Balance	100	190	185
Receipts			
Sales	200	120	110
Total Receipts	200	120	110
Cash Available	300	310	295
Payments			
Purchases	50	60	70
Insurance	30	30	20
Wages	20	25	30
Rent & Rates	10	10	10
Total Payments	110	125	130
Closing Balance	190	185	165

Labels pointing to the table:
- The cash available at the start of the period → Opening Balance
- Money expected to come in → Total Receipts
- Opening balance + receipts → Cash Available
- Money expected to go out → Total Payments
- Cash available less total payments → Closing Balance

We can tell a lot from this cash budget:

Interpretation	Analysis
• Sales are decreasing	This is of concern. The company should find out why sales are expected to decrease (e.g. why is demand going down, is a competitor cheaper or are customers unhappy with the quality of the product?). Market research could find this out. The company might want to increase advertising and promotion to raise awareness of the company and its product.
• Purchases are increasing	This is of concern, especially since sales are forecasted to go down. Perhaps suppliers are intending on increasing their prices, in which case, a cheaper supplier should be found or a discount negotiated. Perhaps too much inventory is being purchased. A JIT approach to inventory management might be a possible solution, depending on the product or service being offered.
• Wages are increasing	This is a concern, especially since sales are forecasted to go down. The company should find out why the wages bill is expected to increase. Perhaps overtime has been offered and this could be reduced. Payment methods could be considered.
• Total payments are increasing	This is because of the reasons above.
• The closing balance each month is decreasing	This is because receipts are decreasing and payments are increasing. A short-term source of finance might be required if this trend continues, to ensure the business can meet its financial obligations.

Individual activity

Amira is the accountant for Stephens Plc and has prepared a cash budget for October–December. She has asked you to prepare a short report on her projected financial position by:

- Identifying areas of concern and/or strength.
- Analysing what might have caused those areas of concern and/or strength.
- Recommending what could be done to improve the financial situation of Stephens Plc with justifications.

 ⚠ Watch point

You need to be able to interpret a cash budget and provide solutions to cash flow problems.

	£ October	£ November	£ December
Opening Balance	2000	1200	−150
Receipts			
Sales	4800	4600	4400
Total Receipts			
Cash Available	6800	5800	4250
Payments			
Purchases	2000	2100	2200
Insurance	400	400	400
Wages	2500	2750	2750
Loan Repayment	200	200	200
Advertising	500	500	500
Purchase of Machine	0	0	6000
Total Payments	5600	5950	12050
Closing Balance	1200	−150	−7800

 Skills

- Information handling
- Applying
- Analysing & evaluating

❓ Questions

1. Describe the purpose of a cash budget.
2. Explain the benefits of preparing a cash budget.
3. Describe the consequences of poor cash flow.
4. Justify actions that could be taken to improve cash flow.

Financial statements

Organisations must prepare a set of financial statements every year. These are the:

- income statement
- statement of financial position.

The financial statements provide a summary of the different financial transactions that have taken place over the last 12 months.

Income statement

This shows a summary of the money that has came in and gone out of the organisation over the past financial year. It shows the **Gross Profit** and **Profit for the Year**.

The amount of money made from buying and selling (**Sales** less **Cost of Sales**)

Items that need to be paid for.

The profit made after expenses have been subtracted from the Gross Profit. (It could be a net loss.)

Income statement for Real Fitness Plc for the year ending 31 December 2019		
	£000	£000
Sales Revenue		300
Lest Cost of Sales		
Opening Inventory	40	
Add Purchases	150	
	190	
Less Closing Inventory	20	
Cost of Sales		170
GROSS PROFIT		130
Less Expenses:		
Rent	10	
Advertising	8	
Electricity	3	
Telephone	15	
Wages	10	46
PROFIT FOR THE YEAR		84

Case study

A summary of the financial position of Real Fitness Plc for the past three years is given below.

	2017 £000	2018 £000	2019 £000
Sales	300	280	260
Gross Profit	130	110	110
Expenses	46	52	55
Profit for the Year	84	58	55

Interpretation	Analysis
• Sales are decreasing	This is of concern. The company should find out why sales have decreased over the three-year period. (For example, why is demand going down, is a competitor cheaper or are customers unhappy with the quality of the product?) Market research could find this out. The company might want to increase advertising and promotion to raise awareness of the company and its product.
• Gross profit has decreased then levelled off	Gross profit has decreased at the same time as sales have decreased; this is to be expected. However, in Year 3, gross profit has remained the same yet sales have decreased. This would indicate that the cost of sales (e.g. purchases) was too high in Year 2 in comparison to sales.
• Expenses are increasing	Expenses have increased yet sales have decreased at the same time. This is of concern. The company should investigate why expenses are increasing and take action where necessary (e.g. seek alternatives).
• Profit for the year is decreasing	This is of concern but is to be expected in light of the points above. The profit for the year took its steepest decrease from Year 1 to Year 2 and not so much in Year 3, which is positive. When the financial statements for Year 4 are published, they might reveal that the situation is more stable.

Make the link

Customers can pay for their purchases through contactless methods, e.g. by using a debit or credit card, or by using Apple Pay.

Statement of financial position

The **statement of financial position** shows the value (worth) of an organisation at a particular point in time. It shows what the organisation owns (assets) and what debts (liabilities) it has. It could be used by a lender to determine whether the organisation is likely to be a risk to them if they loaned them money.

Items owned by the organisation that will last for longer than one year.

Items of short-term worth to the organisation, normally less than a year.

Liabilities are debts. Current liabilities are short-term debts. Non-current liabilities are long-term debts.

Current Assets less Current Liabilities. It shows how easily an organisation can pay its short-term debts.

Shows how the business has been financed (e.g. share equity – the value of shares sold).

Payment to shareholders for having shares.

People who owe the business money having bought goods on credit.

People who the organisation owes money to (e.g. a supplier).

The value of the business at the end of the financial year.

Statement of financial position for Real Fitness Plc as at 31 December 2019		
	£000	£000
NON-CURRENT ASSETS		
Property		250
Equipment		100
Vehicles		<u>50</u>
		400
CURRENT ASSETS		
Closing Inventory	20	
Trade Receivables	40	
Bank	<u>50</u>	
	110	
Less Current Liabilities		
Trade Payables	25	
Working Capital		85
Capital Employed		<u>**485**</u>
Equity		
Share Capital		420
Add Profit for the Year		<u>84</u>
		504
Less Dividends		<u>19</u>
		<u>**485**</u>

Case study

A summary of the financial position of Real Fitness Plc for the past 3 years is given below.

	2017 £000	2018 £000	2019 £000
Non-Current Assets	380	380	400
Current Assets	125	130	110
Current Liabilities	45	40	25
Capital Employed	460	470	485
Equity	475	480	504
Dividends	15	10	19

Interpretation	Analysis
• Value of non-current assets increased	This is positive provided the business has adequate cash flow to pay its short-term debts. The working capital figure (current assets less current liabilities) would confirm that this is satisfactory.
• Value of current assets has been variable	The value of current assets has not remained constant over the three-year period. It is lower in 2019 than in 2018, but 2018 is higher than 2017. The company should monitor this in 2020 to ensure that a decrease does not become the trend.
• Value of current liabilities has decreased	This is positive as the company's short-term debts have decreased over the three-year period. The company has enough working capital to pay its short-term debts.
• Worth of the business (capital employed) is increasing	This is positive as the company is worth more money.
• Dividend payments have not been consistent	The value of dividends has not been consistent over the three-year period. They are higher in 2019 compared to 2018 and this will have pleased shareholders.

Make the link

Specialist software packages (e.g. SAGE) can be used to record financial transactions and then to generate different financial statements.

Individual activity

Amira is the accountant for Stephens Plc and has provided you with a copy of the financial statements of this company for the past three years. She has asked you to prepare a short report:

- identifying areas of concern and/or strength
- analysing what might have caused areas of concern and/or strength
- recommending what could be done to improve the financial situation of Stephens Plc, with justifications.

Income statement

	2017 £000	2018 £000	2019 £000
Sales Revenue	320	340	300
Gross Profit	120	130	120
Expenses	65	75	85
Profit for the Year	55	55	35

Statement of financial position

	2017 £000	2018 £000	2019 £000
Non-Current Assets	580	580	550
Current Assets	235	220	200
Current Liabilities	155	145	135
Capital Employed	660	655	615
Equity	695	695	665
Dividends	35	40	50

Skills

- Information handling
- Applying
- Analysing & evaluating

? Questions

1. Describe the purpose of an income statement.
2. Describe the purpose of a statement of financial position.
3. Define the following terms:
   - gross profit
   - profit for the year
   - trade receivables
   - trade payables
   - working capital
   - dividends
4. Give two examples of a current asset.
5. Give two examples of a current liability.
6. Give two examples of an expense.
7. How are plcs funded?
8. Give examples of when technology could be used by the finance department.

GO! Paired activity

Ask your Teacher/Lecturer for the name of a current accounting software package. Do some research into this package and find out:
- the purpose of the package
- the tasks that it can carry out
- the benefits of using the package
- the costs of adopting this package.

Be prepared to feed back to the rest of your class.

Y Skills

- Applying
- Analysing & evaluating

GO! Group activity

Look at different companies' websites and find their annual report and financial statements. These are real examples of financial statements for plcs.

Y Skills

- Applying

⚠ Make the link

Specialist software packages can be used to record financial information and to generate reports.

Ratios

Accounting information can be analysed in more detail by carrying out **ratio analysis.** Ratio analysis can be used to compare an organisation's performance with its own past, that of similar organisations and also against the industry average. It can help to identify trends and/or irregularities over a period of time. When the results of ratio analysis give cause for concern, action can be taken to try and improve the ratio.

There are lots of different ratios that can be calculated, but in this course we will only look at a few of them.

Ratios can be grouped into different categories depending on whether they provide information on profitability, liquidity or efficiency.

Watch point

It is important to be able to describe the benefits of ratio analysis.

Category	What is it?	Ratios
Profitability	Measure of how profitable the organisation is. These ratios are used to analyse the organisation's expenses, cost of inventory and the selling price.	• Gross profit ratio • Profit for the year ratio • Return on equity employed ratio
Liquidity	Measure of how able the organisation is to pay its short-term debts. These ratios would indicate if an organisation needed to arrange additional finance to pay its bills.	• Current ratio • Acid test ratio
Efficiency	Measure of how well the equity invested into the company is being utilised and if the organisation is performing as efficiently as it can.	• Rate of inventory turnover ratio

Profitability ratios

Gross profit ratio

This ratio shows the profit made from buying and selling inventory.

$$\frac{\text{Gross profit}}{\text{Sales}} \times 100 = \underline{\hspace{1cm}} \%$$

Watch point

Make sure you can describe different types of ratios.

The higher the % the better. If in Year 1 the ratio was 30% and in Year 2 it was 35%, this would show that for every pound made from sales, more of it is gross profit in Year 2 than in Year 1.

Interpretation	Why would it change?
INCREASE in ratio from one year to the next	• Selling price has been raised. • Cost of sales has been lower because cheaper suppliers have been used. • Increase in marketing activities has caused demand to increase. • Better quality product being sold compared to a competitor and this has increased sales.
DECREASE in ratio from one year to the next	• Cost of sales has increased (cheaper suppliers should be located). • Inventory might have been lost due to waste or theft. • Fewer marketing activities might have caused demand to decrease. • Fewer sales due to a better product being sold by a competitor.

Profit for the year ratio

This ratio shows the profit made once expenses have been deducted.

$$\frac{\text{Profit for the year}}{\text{Sales}} \times 100 = \underline{\quad} \%$$

The higher the % the better. If in Year 1 the ratio was 25% and in Year 2 it was 30%, this would show that for every pound made from sales, more of it is net profit in Year 2 than in Year 1.

Interpretation	Why would it change?
INCREASE in ratio from one year to the next	• Gross profit has been higher. • Expenses have been lower (possibly because cheaper alternatives have been sourced).
DECREASE in ratio from one year to the next	• Gross profit has gone down. • Expenses have increased (the organisation should source cheaper alternatives).

Return on equity employed

This ratio shows the return on the equity investment made by the owner or shareholder in the organisation.

$$\frac{\text{Profit for the year}}{\text{Opening equity}} \times 100 = \underline{\hspace{2cm}} \%$$

The higher the % the better. If in Year 1 the ratio was 20% and in Year 2 it was 25%, this would show that in Year 2 a return of 25% has been made. For every £1 invested, a return of 25p has been gained. (NB not dividend.)

Interpretation	Why would it change?
INCREASE in ratio from one year to the next (higher return)	• Sales have increased (due to reasons given for the gross profit ratio). • Expenses have been lower.
DECREASE in ratio from one year to the next (lower return)	• Sales have decreased (due to reasons given for the gross profit ratio). • Expenses have been higher.

Liquidity ratios

Current ratio (also known as the working capital ratio)

This ratio shows how able an organisation is to pay its short-term debts. It would indicate if additional finance is required to pay bills.

$$\frac{\text{Current assets}}{\text{Current liabilities}} : 1$$

An ideal ratio is 2:1. This means that it has double the amount of current assets compared to current liabilities. If the ratio was lower than 2:1 the organisation could struggle to pay its short-term debts. If the ratio is higher than 2:1 the organisation should consider how it would decrease this to ensure it is using its resources in the most effective way.

Interpretation	Why would it change?
INCREASE in ratio from one year to the next	• Current liabilities have decreased (e.g. fewer trade payables). • Current assets have increased (e.g. more inventory or more money in the bank).
DECREASE in ratio from one year to the next	• Current liabilities have increased (e.g. more trade payables). • Current assets have decreased (e.g. less inventory or less money in the bank).

Acid test ratio

This ratio shows how able an organisation is to pay its short-term debts without having to sell its inventory. This is because inventory can be difficult to turn into cash quickly.

$$\frac{\text{Current assets}}{\text{Current liabilities}} : 1$$

A ratio of 1:1 is considered acceptable. This is because it indicates the organisation can pay its short-term debts without having to rely on selling inventory.

Interpretation	Why would it change?
INCREASE in ratio from one year to the next	• Current liabilities have decreased (e.g. fewer trade payables). • Current assets have increased (e.g. more inventory or more money in the bank).
DECREASE in ratio from one year to the next	• Current liabilities have increased (e.g. more trade payables). • Current assets have decreased (e.g. less inventory or less money in the bank).

Efficiency ratios

Rate of inventory turnover

This ratio measures the length of time inventory is held. If inventory is held for a long time, this could suggest that inventory levels are too high. Alternatively, if inventory is only held for a short period of time, it might be because a JIT approach is used or because the re-order inventory level is low. The type of product being sold will also influence whether it is held for a long or short period of time.

Make the link

Inventory management systems are covered on page 99–102.

$$\frac{\text{Cost of sales}}{\text{Average inventory}^*} = \text{'times'}$$

*Average inventory = closing inventory + opening inventory / 2

Interpretation	Why would it change?
INCREASE in ratio from one year to the next	• Increase in the cost of sales (e.g. purchases). • Decrease in average inventory holding.
DECREASE in ratio from one year to the next	• Decrease in the cost of sales (e.g. purchases). • Increase in average inventory holding.

Problems with ratios

There are some problems or limitations with carrying out ratio analysis. Organisations that carry out ratio analysis need to be aware that:

- the figures used to calculate the ratios are historic and do not show what could happen in the future

- comparisons between different organisations are difficult because the results are only useful when compared with an organisation of the same size and type

- external factors (PESTEC – see page 33) are not taken into consideration

- the results do not consider any workforce-related issues such as staff motivation or morale

- new product development or launches are not considered.

Group activity

Make a list of how technology could be used in the finance department. Think about the use of:

- spreadsheets
- PowerPoint presentations
- databases
- word processors
- banking apps
- e-mail
- videoconferencing

Skills

- Applying

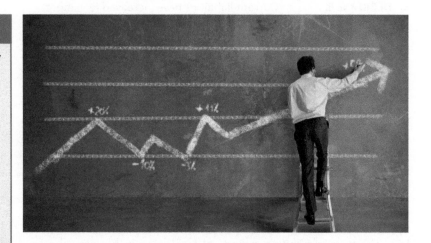

Case study

A summary of the ratio analysis of Real Fitness Plc for the past three years is given below.

	2017 £000	2018 £000	2019 £000
Gross Profit Ratio	58%	62%	65%
Profit for the Year Ratio	34%	32%	30%
Return on Equity Employed Ratio	15%	12%	10%
Current Ratio	1.8:1	2.5:1	2:1
Acid Test Ratio	0.88:1	0.78:1	0.56:1
Inventory Turnover Ratio	3.2 times	3.1 times	3 times

Interpretation	Analysis
• Gross profit ratio has increased over the three years	This could be because the selling price has been raised and has resulted in more gross profit. It could also be because cost of sales (purchases) has been lower due to finding a new supplier.
• Profit for the year ratio has decreased over the three years	This is because expenses have increased – not cost of sales otherwise the gross profit ratio would have decreased and it hasn't. The organisation should seek cheaper alternatives to lower its expenses, e.g. cheaper electricity provider.
• Return on equity employd has decreased over the three years	This means shareholders are not receiving as much of a return on their investment. This is likely to be because expenses have increased as shown by the decrease in the profit for the year ratio.
• Current ratio has been variable over the past three years	The ideal ratio is 2:1 and has been this or greater in all years except 2017. However, given the fact that the ratio in 2018 and 2019 is positive, this should be monitored to ensure that it remains around 2:1.
• Acid test ratio has decreased over the past three years	An ideal ratio is 1:1 and it has been below this in all three years and continues to decrease. This means the organisation does not have enough current assets to pay its short-term debts without having to resort to selling inventory.
• Inventory turnover ratio has decreased over the three years	There has been a decrease in the cost of sales, as confirmed by the increase in the gross profit ratio.

Individual activity

Amira is the accountant for Stephens Plc and has provided you with a copy of the ratios for the company for the past three years. She has asked you to prepare a short report:

- identifying trends in the ratios given
- analysing what might have caused ratios to increase or decrease
- recommending what could be done to improve each ratio of Stephens Plc, with justifications.

	2017 £000	2018 £000	2019 £000
Gross Profit Ratio	66%	63%	60%
Profit for the Year Ratio	28%	30%	32%
Return on Equity Employed Ratio	22%	13%	16%
Current Ratio	2.4:1	2.2:1	1:9
Acid Test Ratio	0.7:1	0.6:1	0.5:1
Inventory Turnover Ratio	4.8 times	4.4 times	4 times

 Skills

- Information handling
- Applying
- Analysing & evaluating

★ Key questions

1. Describe and justify sources of finance appropriate for large organisations.
2. Describe the purpose of financial statements.
3. Describe accounting ratios and outline the use or limitations of ratio analysis.

Summary

This chapter provided you with an overview of the finance function and the purpose and content of different financial statements. Sources of finance and ratio analysis were also explored. The use of technology to carry out different activities in the finance department was also indicated.

The main topics in this chapter were:

- Sources of finance
- Cash budgeting
- Financial statements
- Ratios
- Technology in finance

By successfully answering the key questions, you will show that you have grasped the main topics covered in this chapter.

6 END OF CHAPTER MATERIAL

Sample exam question

Make sure you read each exam question carefully as every word is there for a reason. It is good practice to break each question down into parts before you answer it so that you know what is required.

For example:

Justify sources of finance that could be used to expand a business. (6 marks)

> The command word – NB justify means to give reasons for something.

> This is a strategic (long-term) decision, so therefore only sources of finance suitable for long-term uses are appropriate.

Sample answer

Additional shares could be issued to existing or new shareholders because large amounts of capital can be obtained this way **(1 justify mark)**. It also does not have to be paid back (unlike loans that have interest) **(1 justify mark)**. If the expansion abroad is not successful, this source gives shareholders limited liability **(1 justify mark)**. The company could also consider leasing equipment abroad to save them having to outlay large sums of cash for machinery and this will help to improve cash flow **(1 justify mark)**. It also means the company will be able to keep equipment up-to-date as they will not have to pay large sums of money to have the equipment placed or upgraded **(1 justify mark)**. A bank loan could also be obtained from the bank. This is normally easy to arrange and can be done quickly **(1 justify mark)**.

Examiner's comments

The candidate has justified the use of three different sources of finance (additional share issue, leasing equipment and a bank loan). They have given different reasons why each source of finance would be suitable (i.e. they have justified them). **(6/6 marks)**

More sample exam questions

- Explain the benefits and costs of issuing additional shares. (4 marks)
- Justify the use of crowd funding. (3 marks)
- Describe causes of cash flow problems. (5 marks)
- Justify methods of solving cash flow problems. (5 marks)
- Justify the use of a spreadsheet in the finance department. (4 marks)
- Discuss the purpose of different financial statements. (6 marks)
- Discuss the use of modern technology in finance. (6 marks)
- Explain the purpose of ratio analysis. (4 marks)
- Discuss the limitations of ratio analysis. (6 marks)
- Describe the purpose of profitability ratios. (4 marks)
- Justify actions that could be taken to improve liquidity ratios. (3 marks)

Check your progress

	HELP NEEDED	GETTING THERE	CONFIDENT
Role of finance	◯	◯	◯
Sources of finance	◯	◯	◯
Cash budgeting	◯	◯	◯
Income statement	◯	◯	◯
Statement of financial position	◯	◯	◯
Ratio analysis	◯	◯	◯
Technology in finance	◯	◯	◯

Case study answers

H&M case study (page 25)

1. Behaving in a responsible way towards, for example, employees and the planet.

2. Code of Conduct

3. The standards expected of any supplier or organisation working with H&M.

4. 100% Leading the Change – driving innovation, promoting transparency, praising sustainable activities. 100% Circular & Climate Positive – committed to using only recycled or raw materials that are sustainably sourced. 100% Fair & Work – valuing diversity, safe working conditions, treated fairly.

5. They will get a poor image and therefore might lose customers. Employees might not want to work for H&M and therefore would struggle to have staff to provide a service.

Morrisons case study (page 31)

1. Market share – number of customers/sales revenue generated from a market.

2. To increase sales and profit, which in turn will increase the return on investment for owners (e.g. dividends for shareholders). To increase the number of customers, which will increase profits and market share, and may enable the organisation to become a market leader. To take advantage of economies of scale (discounts for bulk buying), therefore reducing costs. To become bigger with the intention that it will reduce risk of a takeover by another organisation. To gain a better reputation in the marketplace which will encourage new customers to buy, therefore increasing sales and ultimately profit.

3. Increase the number of stores.

   Increase the number of employees.

   Increase online presence.

   Enter new markets.

4. Business will gain a greater market share and will reduce the number of competitors in the market. As a result of fewer competitors, higher prices could be charged by the business. It also allows the business to gain economies of scale, which will in turn lower production costs and increase profit.

5. **Backward vertical** – by taking over a supplier it means that the business should have sufficient supplies available at reasonable prices, as they will not need to add the element of profit to raw materials. As the business now has control over inputs, quality can be more readily assured. They may also be able to limit the supply of input inventory being supplied to competitors.

   Forward vertical – by taking over a customer this will mean that supplies are readily available to the shop, helping to ensure regular sales.

6. To gain a good reputation/image, to increase the number of customers/sales, to gain positive media attention.

Premier Inn case study (page 46)

1. Environmental (awareness of and acting responsibility towards the environment and planet) and social (changes in values/beliefs and trends).

2. Environmental – diverting 100% of waste to landfill, cutting carbon emissions in half, sourcing beef and milk from UK and Ireland, using responsible suppliers. Social – sourcing beef and milk from the UK and Ireland, commitment to employing a range of people regardless of who they are or where they are from, investing in skills, charity activities.

3. Premier Inn wants to employ people from a variety of backgrounds and employees need Premier inn to provide them with relevant skills and training. Premier Inn needs its suppliers to supply good quality materials at reasonable prices and its suppliers need Premier Inn to purchase from them.

4. Premier Inn wants to maximise profit by seeking suppliers who provide products at reasonable costs, whereas suppliers want to maximise profit by charging as much as they can. Customers want value for money rooms whereas Premier Inn want to maximise profit. Employees want a high return for their labour, whereas Premier inn want to minimise costs and maximise profit.

5. Commitment to reducing carbon emissions by 50%, sourcing UK beef and milk, diverting 100% to landfill, charity fundraising.

6. Organic growth – growing internally by expanding the number of rooms/hotels. This method can be safer than taking over or merging with other existing companies.

FirstGroup Plc case study (page 114)

1. To meet its aim of being socially responsible, to gain a good image/reputation, to gain positive media attention, to increase sales.

2. Reusing parts from buses rather than sending to landfill, recycling old uniforms, reducing the number of timetables it is producing, encouraging customers to print their own timetables.

3. Reusing parts from buses - cuts down on the volume of parts being sent to landfill and the number of journeys that would need to be made to take old buses to landfill. Recycling old uniforms – saves energy being used in disposing of these and/or decreases volume being sent to landfill. Also shows a social commitment towards the charity. Reducing the number of timetables it is producing – reduction in volume to be transported (reduces carbon emissions), reduction in paper being used in production, reduction in energy needed to produce timetables. Also reduces costs (and therefore increases profitability). Encouraging customers to print their own timetables – reduces costs to FirstGroup and also the volume of timetables it needs to produce.

Answers to questions

Chapter 2: Understanding Business

PAGE 12

1. Primary – businesses in the primary sector extract raw materials from the ground. These businesses include agriculture, fishing, oil and gas extraction, and mining.

   Secondary – businesses in this sector manufacture goods. They take raw materials and transform them into a tangible, finished product. Examples include shipbuilding, breweries and builders.

   Tertiary – businesses in the tertiary sector provide a service, an intangible product. The service is provided by people who have been trained to offer it. Examples include fitness instructors, hotels, supermarkets, hairdressers and health care providers.

   Quaternary – businesses in the quaternary sector provide a knowledge-based and information service and are often concerned with innovation, research and development. This includes consultancy, ICT and computing, education, scientific research and financial services. People working in the quaternary sector are highly skilled.

2. Wealth is created by a business by adding value to a product as it goes through the production process.

3. Gross domestic product – the value of all the goods and services produced in the UK.

4. **Benefits**
   - Jobs are created and therefore this reduces the UK's unemployment figure.
   - When people become employed, they might have access to training and the opportunity to learn new skills.
   - As a result of less unemployment, demand for goods and services increases and the standard of living increases.
   - Tax is paid by businesses and individuals when they have a job and this money is paid to the Government that can then invest this money into different Government services, e.g. health, police and education.
   - Other businesses will be keen to invest.
   - Infrastructure (e.g. access to utilities such as water and electricity) can be improved and roads and transport links can be improved.

   Costs
   - Businesses can have a large environmental impact on a country or specific location (e.g. noise and traffic pollution or an increase in wastage).
   - The volume of non-renewable resources, e.g. oil, can decrease.
   - Greenfield sites, land that has previously been unused or used for agriculture, is lost – however, this could be seen as an advantage.
   - Too much demand for goods and services can cause inflation; this is when the price of goods and services rises and people may no longer be able to afford to purchase some products.

PAGE 22

1. Private limited company shareholders have to be invited to become shareholders whereas with a public limited company, shares are available to anyone in the stock market. Both are private sector businesses.

2. **Benefits**

   - Limited liability for the shareholders of the company (this means if the company was to go bankrupt, shareholders would only lose the money they invested into the company and not their own personal assets). This also means that shareholders may be more likely to invest in the company.
   - Large amounts of capital (finance) can be raised by selling more shares via the stock exchange and lenders may feel more confident in investing in larger companies.
   - Can often take advantage of economies of scale because of their size; this means they can obtain discounts for buying in bulk, e.g. raw materials.
   - Plcs can control more of the market compared to smaller organisations and therefore have more power within it.

   Costs

   - Financial statements have to be published annually that will involve a cost in producing them.
   - There is no control over who can buy shares in the company.
   - Company has to abide by the Company Act to avoid legal action being taken.
   - Profits may be lower when the company is initially set up due to high start-up costs.

3. A person who starts a business and provides a good or service supplied by another business (the franchisor) is known as a franchisee and operates a business known as a franchise.

4. **Benefits**

   - Income is guaranteed as the franchisee normally pays a percentage of profit each year to the franchisor.
   - If the business does not work, the cost of failure is split and therefore risk is shared.
   - Market share of the whole franchise is increasing when more branches are being opened.

   Costs

   - As only a percentage of turnover is given to the franchisor by the franchisee, this might be lower than what the franchisor could have earned themselves.
   - A franchisee could damage the reputation and image of the business and this could cause problems for the whole franchise.

5. **Benefits**

   - They can set up a business using a business name that is well established and that people are familiar with. This could allow them to gain customers and sales quickly compared to setting up a brand new business. It also reduces the risk of failure.
   - Advertising costs are paid for by the franchisor, which saves the franchisee having to spend money on this themselves.
   - Franchisor carries out training for the whole business and therefore it is appropriate to the needs of the workforce and will save the franchisee money.

Costs

- It requires a considerable sum of money to set up a franchise and the franchisee may not have this money available.
- The franchisee might have little or no control over the products available, their price or the layout of the store. The franchisee might find this frustrating as they cannot inject any new ideas into the business.
- Some of the profit earned has to be given to the franchisor, therefore reducing the money that the franchisee earns.

6. Benefits

- Economies of scale can be taken advantage of, therefore reducing costs.
- Legal restrictions can be avoided in other countries compared to the home country.
- May be able to take advantage of different tax regulations in other countries, therefore increasing profitability.
- Expanding abroad will mean the organisation becomes bigger, increasing sales and also safer from takeovers by other organisations.
- Government grants might be given in some countries for locating there that do not require to be paid back.
- Resources, e.g. labour, might be cheaper in some countries, reducing the overall amount spent on expenses.

Costs

- Each country's laws will need to be complied with – this might mean changes need to be made to the good or service that might be expensive.
- The culture in each country might vary from one to another and the organisation will need to consider this.
- Language barriers may make trading more difficult and expensive if language interpreters need to be employed.
- Language barriers may also mean that communication is misinterpreted and decisions wrongly made.

7. Providing jobs, not polluting the environment (e.g. recycling what it can), respecting home laws.

8.
- Language differences – trading might be more difficult.
- Cultural differences – different cultures might need to be respected, e.g. customers and employees.
- Cheaper labour – higher profitability, lower expenses.
- Different tax rates – might be lower, resulting in higher profitability.
- Raw materials could be more easily accessed, lowering costs.

9. National Government controls what happens in the UK and makes decisions impacting on the whole of the UK. In Scotland, we also have a Scottish Government that has devolved responsibility from the House of Commons for certain things, e.g. education and health. Local governments make decisions and control budgets for the local area, e.g. Glasgow City Council.

10. Third sector businesses:

- Charities are owned and controlled by a Board of Trustees. They are regulated by the Government and the income they make is put towards a specific cause.

- Social Enterprises have a main social or environmental aim rather than to make profit for owners or shareholders, but are run in a business-like way.

11. Public limited companies are owned by shareholders, whereas public sector organisations are owned by the Government/taxpayer. Public limited companies are controlled by a Board of Directors, whereas public sector organisations are controlled by the Scottish Government and the relevant Minister.

PAGE 32

1. **Private sector**

   - To maximise profit
   - To satisfy shareholders
   - To provide high quality products

   Public sector

   - To provide a service to communities
   - To keep within budgets

   Third sector

   - To help a specific cause
   - To raise donations

   All businesses (regardless of sector) might have the objective of being socially responsible.

2. **Private sector**

   - To maximise profit – to ensure dividend payments are made to shareholders.
   - To satisfy shareholders – to ensure they continue to invest into the company.
   - To provide high quality products – to satisfy customers.

   Public sector

   - To provide a service to communities – to ensure communities get what they need.
   - To keep within budgets – to ensure they break even and don't have a budget deficit.

   Third sector

   - To help a specific cause, e.g. to relieve poverty or to provide a service to communities.
   - To raise donations – to help ensure maximum benefit is given.

3. Horizontal integration – two businesses providing the same service or producing the same good join together (e.g. two airlines joining together).

   When businesses in the same industry, but which operate at different stages of production, join together this is called vertical integration. This cuts out the middlemen involved with two separate businesses and therefore cuts costs. There are two types of vertical integration:

   - Backward vertical integration – taking over a supplier.
   - Forward vertical integration – taking over a customer.

   Diversification is when two businesses that provide different goods and services join together. It is also referred to as a conglomerate.

A takeover is when one large business takes control and ownership of a smaller one.

A merger is when two businesses of approximately the same size agree to become one.

Organic growth happens when the business increases the number of goods and services it offers or increases the number of branches/outlets and employees that it has. This will help to increase sales and profit.

Deintegration (or demerger) occurs when a business splits into two or more separate businesses.

Divestment is when a business sells off some of its assets or smaller parts of the business to raise finance.

4. It will reduce risk of failure by operating in more than one market and will also allow profit to be obtained from more than one market.

5. The parts of the business that are sold off are normally less profitable and this finance can be put back into the business.

6. Manager might put their own objectives before the organisation.

7. • To encourage customer loyalty
   • To gain a good reputation

PAGE 40

1. Things outwith the control of an organisation that impact on how it operates.

2. Any two from each table given on pages 34–40.

3. • Changes to economic policy may increase consumers' buying power, therefore increasing demand for a business.
   • Changes to an economic policy might restrict the ability of banks to lend money and this may cause a cash flow problem.

4. Positive and negative impacts of different environmental influences are given on page 39.

5. • To remain competitive
   • For planning purposes
   • To make decisions
   • To ensure survival
   • To maximise profit

6. • 5G – 5G is the most recent mobile connectivity to be rolled out across the UK, beginning with several major cities in 2019. It provides faster connectivity and data transfer speeds.
   • Machine learning – The study of algorithms (rules) and statistical models that allows a computer to learn and perform tasks and follow instructions without being explicitly told what to do.
   • Augmented reality – This technology provides interactive, reality-based displays that includes text, sounds and graphics. It gives the user the feeling they are in the actual location or environment.
   • 2FA – Providing two forms of authentication to access a system or application.

7. • Try to find an alternative lender that may have cheaper rates.
   • Carry out market research and then provide customers with the fashion that they want.
   • May have to change location.

8. Answers may include having to retrain staff, greater use of the gig economy, creating and developing applications, allowing customers access to services rather than them owning them.

PAGE 43

1. The availability of finance, the quality and skills of employees, the experience and skills of managers to make decisions, the availability of appropriate technology to carry out tasks.

2. The values, beliefs and norms that are shared among members of an organisation.

3. Employees feel they are part of and belong to an organisation, which can motivate them; motivated staff will lead to improved efficiency and higher productivity; positive relationships within the organisation may exist, which results in better communication; employee loyalty can be increased, which will decrease staff turnover.

4. The vision and aims of the organisation, the opinion and views of employees, the design of stores/logos/uniforms, the organisation's procedures.

PAGE 51

1. • Size of the organisation (e.g. larger organisations tend to require a more formal structure compared to smaller ones).
   • The technology being used (e.g. this could be used to communicate with other parts of the organisations in other locations).
   • Who the customer is (in other words, the target market).
   • The good or service that is being provided.
   • The amount of finance available to the organisation (e.g. this might limit the type of structure or grouping that could be used).

2. • Who has overall **responsibility** for the organisation.
   • The different levels of **authority** and **responsibility** within the organisation.
   • The lines of **communication** and the **chain of command**.
   • The **span of control** for different managers.
   • Different **relationships** that exist within the organisation.
   • Where work could be **delegated** to **subordinates**.

3. • Delegation – giving the authority and responsibility to someone else to carry out a particular task.
   • Chain of command – this shows how instructions are passed down through an organisation and how communication can flow up and down the organisation.
   • Authority – having power to make decisions.
   • Responsibility – being answerable for decisions and actions taken within the organisation.

4. Human resources, finance, operations, research & development, marketing

5. Comparison of any two structures from page 49–50.

6. • The needs of customers within each specific location can be catered for.
   • The organisation can become familiar with different cultures that exist in different locations.

7. • People can contact specific departments if they require specialist advice or help (e.g. Marketing might contact HR when recruiting a new employee for that department).
   • Clear lines of authority exist (as shown on the organisation chart) between subordinates
   • Managers and other employees will usually have clearly defined tasks and duties to carry out.

8. Products can be marketed towards each specific customer group. The organisation can build up loyalty with their customers because activities are focused on the specific customer group, and therefore a higher level of customer service is achieved.

9. Specialised knowledge of each product is gained by each department, resulting in a higher quality product. Changes in the business environment can be responded to quickly, which allows it to remain competitive.

10. Product grouping focuses on a specific product (which maybe bought by a range of customers), whereas customer grouping focuses on a specific customer (who may buy a range of products).

PAGE 55

1. Wide span of control means there are many subordinates whereas a narrow span of control means few subordinates.

2. • More empowerment is possible due to the number of subordinates.
   • Tasks can be delegated more easily to the subordinate most suitably skilled to carry these out; however, employees may feel reluctant and uncomfortable with this.
   • As there are a large number of subordinates, this can cause extra stress for the manager who may have little time to deal with staff-related issues.
   • Managers may feel that, as they have more subordinates to manage they are more powerful and this can be motivating to them.
   • The organisation will have fewer managers and therefore save money.
   • A shorter chain of command will exist and therefore communication and decision-making is likely to be more effective.

3. Subordinates are more likely to have the chance to participate in decision-making and planning. However, a long chain of command will exist and therefore communication and decision-making might be slower.

4. A tall structure has many layers/levels whereas a flat structure has fewer. A tall structure has a long chain of command whereas a flat structure has a shorter chain of command.

5. • Matrix (or project-based) structures tend to be formed when a specific task or project is to be carried out.
   • People from across the organisation will come together from various departments to form the matrix structure.
   • When the task or project has been completed, the matrix structure will become obsolete.
   • A project or team leader will be appointed to provide leadership to the task or project being undertaken.

- Because people from across the organisation may participate in this structure, it can be motivating for employees and useful to the organisation when problems are being solved.
- Even though it gives employees the opportunity to learn new skills by participating in a project or task, it can be costly to implement and for the organisation to coordinate.
- Employees may find having two managers (e.g. from their own functional area as well as for the matrix structure) confusing.

6. **Benefits**

- Suitable for smaller organisations
- Decisions can be made quickly by the owner

Costs

- Little input from employees, lower motivation
- Fewer ideas as employees are not consulted

7. Decisions are made by senior management in a centralised structure whereas they are delegated to departments in a decentralised structure. Employees in a centralised structure are consulted whereas in a decentralised structure they are not. Consistency of decision-making exists in a centralised structure whereas in a decentralised structure this cannot always be the case.

8. See notes on page 54.

9. • Line relationship – this is a relationship between a subordinate and their line manager.

- Lateral relationship – this is a relationship between two or more people on the same level of the organisation.
- Functional relationship – this is a relationship between two functional areas in an organisation, e.g. one providing support to another.
- Staff relationship – this is a relationship between two or more people in an organisation who provide advice or support to others.

10. A formal relationship exists when two people communicate on a formal basis, e.g. because of a line or lateral relationship within the organisation. An informal relationship is when two or more people communicate on an informal basis, perhaps outwith the organisation, e.g. over coffee.

PAGE 57

1. • The size of the organisation has changed.
   - The availability of finance has changed.
   - Market conditions have changed.
   - New technology has become available.

2. Delayering involves removing layers of a structure whereas downsizing involves removing some of the activities from an organisation.

3. • As well as saving money on management salaries, it allows for quicker communication and decision-making because there are fewer layers.
   - Market conditions may be responded to more quickly compared to in a taller structure.
   - Employees may feel more empowered to make decisions and to use their own initiative; this can increase motivation and productivity.

4. Employees may feel more empowered to make decisions and to use their own initiative; this can increase motivation and productivity. This is because managers will have a wider span of control. Ultimately, this might mean that the supervision and management of employees could be more difficult. Delayering also means that there will be fewer promotion opportunities for existing staff.

5. • To enable the organisation to concentrate on core activities.

   • Specialists may carry out the activity on behalf of the organisation.

PAGE 63

1. • Plan – thinking about the future by setting the organisation's objectives and deciding what needs to be done to achieve each objective.
   • Organise – ensuring resources (e.g. human and financial) are available to allow objectives to be achieved.
   • Command – instructing employees to carry out specific tasks so that they know what is expected to achieve objectives.
   • Control – checking and monitoring work and tasks that have been completed to ensure they meet the standard required to achieve objectives. Where necessary, action can be taken to ensure activities are on track to help achieve each objective.
   • Coordinate – ensuring resources (e.g. employees) are in place at the right time and working towards the same objective. This will ensure objectives are achieved as efficiently as they can.
   • Delegate – the responsibility for carrying out a task can be given to someone else (delegated), so that the manager can concentrate on other activities.
   • Motivate – encouraging and inspiring employees to work as hard as they can so that as many objectives are achieved as possible and to the highest standard.

2. • Strategic – long-term decisions setting out the organisation's vision and objectives.
   • Tactical – medium-term decisions putting in place actions to achieve strategic decisions.
   • Operational – short-term decisions concerned with routine and day-to-day tasks.

3. • Strategic – to expand into a new country, to grow, to diversity the product range.
   • Tactical – to find a cheaper supplier, to expand the range of products, to develop a new marketing strategy.
   • Operational – staff working hours, to give someone a day off.

4. • S – strengths – the internal strengths of the organisation.
   • W – weaknesses – the internal weaknesses of the organisation.
   • O – opportunities – the external opportunities available to the organisation.
   • T – threats – the external threats that may impact upon the organisation.

5. • Asking employees for their views, by carrying out a survey or staff meeting, on how well the decision has worked and how effective they think it is.
   • Looking at quantitative information (e.g. productivity rates and sales or profit figures) to see if the decision has impacted negatively or positively.
   • Looking at employee absence rates (again, quantitative information) to see if there has been an increase or decrease in the number of days employees take off work.
   • Measuring the level of employee motivation within the workplace to see whether or not the decision has reduced or increased this.

- Asking customers for their opinion by carrying out research (e.g. conducting a survey) as this will give first-hand information from their opinion.
- Examining the number of complaints received.
- Reviewing online customer reviews on e.g. social media, as well as in the press, for feedback.

6.
- The availability of finance might mean that the most effective option cannot be chosen.
- The number of employees might limit what can or cannot be achieved as there is not enough staff to carry out the decision.
- The skill and training requirements of employees may not be high enough to implement decisions and therefore the decision cannot be implemented.
- The ability and skill of managers to make decisions as more complex decisions will demand more skills from managers.
- The policies and procedures of the organisation might limit what decision can be made and, as a result, the decision might have to be modified to comply with them.
- The quality of information available; a lack of quality information might mean that a fully informed decision cannot be made.
- Employees might be resistant to change, which will make implementing the decision more difficult and time consuming, especially if they disagree with the option chosen.
- Appropriate technology might not be available to implement the best decision and therefore money needs to be spent upgrading technology.

Chapter 3: Management of Marketing

PAGE 71

1.

Segment	What it is
Gender	Segmenting by gender means to market a product towards a specific gender, i.e. male or female.
Age	Segmenting by age means to market a product towards people of a certain age group, e.g. holidays for 18–30 year olds.
Occupation	Segmenting by occupation means to market a product towards people who do a particular job, e.g. stethoscope for doctors.
Religious or cultural belief	Segmenting by religious or cultural belief means to market a product towards people who follow a specific religious or cultural faith.
Income/Social class	Segmenting by income or social class means to market a product towards people who have a certain level of income or belong to a particular social group (e.g. working or upper class).
Geographical location	Segmenting by geographical location means to market a product towards people who live in a particular location, e.g. sun cream for hot locations!
Lifestyle	Segmenting by lifestyle means to market a product towards people who lead a particular life, e.g. if they are into sport and fitness.

2.

Market-led (market orientated)	Product-led (product orientated)
• Product produced based on what the customer wants. • Customer wants and needs are identified through market research. • Changes in social factors (e.g. trends and fashion) can be identified and acted upon more easily. • The market may have significant competition.	• Product produced because the organisation thinks it is good at providing it. • Little or no market research carried out as the needs and wants of the customer are not of importance. • The market may have little or no competition.

3. Differentiated marketing – marketing products towards a particular market segment.
Undifferentiated marketing – focusing on more than one target market.

4. • To develop a successful marketing strategy.
 • To make decisions about the product the organisation offers.

5. • Why do they buy what they do?
 • What motivates them to buy?
 • What influences buying decisions?
 • What type of customer buys the product?
 • Where do they choose to buy? Why?
 • What do they look for when buying?

6.

Impulse purchases	Buying something without thinking, often in the spur of the moment. It might be because something has influenced the customer to buy (e.g. a promotion).
Routine purchases	Buying something because it is habit, e.g. going to buy a loaf of bread. These types of purchases will happen without much thought.
Limited decision-making purchases	Buying something that requires some thought before a decision is made. For example, thinking about whether or not a piece of clothing is appropriate for a certain purpose.
Extensive decision-making purchases	Buying something that requires a high degree of thought before a decision is made. For example, buying a new car or a house. These types of purchases might not be made very often.

7. Electronic point of sale systems (EPOS) can gather information about consumer behaviour that the organisation can attempt to analyse and understand.

- When people make purchases in a supermarket or shop, the EPOS system is collecting data about them and their buying habits.
- Promotions, offers and mailshots can then be designed specifically for them.

PAGE 76

1. Attempting to find out what customers want and what is happening in the marketplace.

It involves looking at existing information and gathering new information.

2. Field research involves gathering new information whereas desk research involves looking at existing information.

3. Websites, newspapers/magazines, government reports, textbooks

4. Surveys, interviews, observations, hall tests, focus groups

5.
- Products can be adapted to meet customer requirements.
- Products can be tested by customers to gain their reactions.
- Information can be used to ensure the correct market segment is being targeted.
- It evaluates how effective a marketing campaign is.

6. Questionnaires – asking people's views and opinions to see whether or not they like something. This is a good way of asking a lot of people for their views, particularly if done online or through the post, and is inexpensive compared to, for example, observations.

Observations – watching people and recording their behaviour towards something. This information can be analysed quickly as it is often quantitative. People usually react naturally as they are often unaware they are being observed.

Hall tests – allowing customers to try out a product. First-hand information is gathered.

Focus groups – a discussion between a selected number of people and a researcher. People's feelings towards different topics can be gathered as a discussion is taking place.

7. Primary information is new information gathered for a specific purpose, whereas secondary information is old information gathered for another purpose.

8. Internal information is information from within the organisation, e.g. sales figures, whereas external information is from outwith the organisation, e.g. Government reports or competitors' websites.

9. • Random sampling – randomly selecting people from a list, e.g. a telephone book. These individuals must then be questioned.

   • Quota sampling – selecting people to question based on certain characteristics, e.g. age, gender or occupation.

10. • Surveys could be created and distributed via a website.

    • Spreadsheets could be used to analyse research data.

    • Analytics from social media websites could be used to establish the success of promotions.

PAGE 80

1. Because organisations are now so closely focused on their customers.

2. • **Process** – the different processes and systems used to deliver the service being provided.
   • **People** – those involved in providing the service to customers, e.g. staff.
   • **Physical evidence** – the location of where the service is being offered and what it looks like, e.g. store layout and design.

3. • Process – for example, the 'drive-thru'.
   • People – staff serving customers.
   • Physical evidence – store layout and design.

4. • Price – promotional pricing could be used to encourage customers.
   • Product – the product could be adapted or changed (e.g. new features added) to make it more appealing to customers.
   • Place – the product could be sold in more locations to make it more accessible.
   • Promotion – advertising methods could be changed or increased to target a wider range of people.

PAGE 84

1. The actual good or service being sold.

2.

Development	Research and development of the product. A number of activities are carried out (e.g. market research, test marketing, prototype is built).
Introduction	Product is launched onto the market. Product is heavily advertised and sales will begin to increase.
Growth	The product has gained greater awareness and sales grow rapidly.
Maturity	Sales are at a peak and the product is well known in the marketplace. Extension strategies might be used at this stage to keep sales at a peak.
Saturation	The end of maturity; everyone has the product and is no longer demanding it. This might be a single point of time or it might be for longer.
Decline	Sales decline as newer and better products are introduced to the market. The product is no longer wanted. Product is eventually withdrawn.

3.

Development	No sales, high costs. No profit.
Introduction	Sales are low and costs are high. Very little or no profit.
Growth	Sales grow rapidly and profit begins to increase.
Maturity	High profits.
Saturation	High profits before they decrease.
Decline	Profits fall and a loss might be incurred eventually.

4. Methods used to try and stimulate sales and encourage people to buy.

5.
- Changing the appearance of the packaging to give the product a new image.
- Changing the size, variety or shape of the product as this makes it different from the original.
- Improving the quality of the finished product by, for example, using higher quality raw materials.
- Changing the method of promotion used to promote the product; for example, by offering a discount.
- Changing the method of advertising the product to reach a larger number of people.
- Changing the price of the product (up or down) to reach a different market segment.
- Changing the place the product is sold, e.g. offering it online as well as in a shop.
- Changing the name of the product.
- Changing the use of the product so that it can be used for different purposes.

6. Range of products being offered.

7. Benefits
- To reduce risk of failure of one product as one product might be doing better than another.
- To appeal to a variety of market segments as different products will appeal to different types of customers.
- To increase sales and profits from selling different products as customers will be able to buy a variety of products from the same business.

- To make introducing a new product easier as customers will already be aware of the business.
- To cope with products that are only demanded in certain seasons as other products will gain sales at different times of the year.

Costs

- Costs of promoting and advertising lots of different products could be high and could result in less profit.
- If one product receives a bad reputation or image, this might impact upon all the products being sold by the business.
- Maintaining a varied product portfolio will involve a high cost of research and development.
- Cost of purchasing and maintaining machinery for different types of products might be high.
- Staff may require training on the features of different products, which could be time consuming and expensive.

8. • Used to plot the range of products offered by an organisation.
   - Shows the position of a product in relation to its market share and whether it is achieving market growth.
   - Four components: problem child/question marks, star, dog, cash cow
   - See diagram on page 83.

PAGE 87

1. The amount charged to the customer to purchase the good or service.

2. Destroyer – this forces competitors out of the market so that the business can then charge higher prices at a later date.

   Skimming – a high price can be charged because little or no competition exists. A large profit can be made.

   Psychological – this method tricks people into thinking the product is cheaper than it is and attracts them to buy it. Attracts consumers who buy on impulse.

   Discrimination – allows a business to vary its price depending on demand at a certain period of time.

   Cost-plus – ensures that the cost of making the product is covered and that a profit is also made.

3. Skimming – a high price can be charged because little or no competition exists.

4. Premium pricing – the high price gives the product a unique and exclusive image.

5. • The life cycle of the product.
   - The price charged by competitors.
   - How much it costs to make the product.
   - How much profit is wanted.
   - How much of the product can be supplied.
   - The market segment that the product is focused towards.

6. To remain competitive.

PAGE 92

1. Channel of distribution is the route a product will follow to get from the manufacturer to the customer.

2.
   - The actual product and its life cycle.
   - The image and exclusivity the manufacturer wants the product to have.
   - The availability of finance.
   - The reputation and reliability of wholesalers and retailers.
   - Legal restrictions.
   - The logistic facilities available by the manufacturer (how able it is to transport and store the product from one place to the next).

3.
   - A wholesaler buys large quantities of items from the manufacturer and then sells them on to retailers, or directly to the customer, in smaller quantities.
   - A retailer is an organisation that distributes products to the customer on behalf of the manufacturer.

4.

Benefits	Costs
<ul><li>Distribution and storage costs are reduced because products might be bought in bulk.</li><li>The wholesaler may promote the manufactured product, resulting in less cost for the manufacturer.</li><li>Risk of not selling the product to a retailer or to the customer is taken on by the wholesaler and therefore risk for the manufacturer is reduced.</li><li>Packaging, labelling and marketing might be carried out by the wholesaler.</li><li>The manufacturer does not have to worry about having to sell excess inventory if there are changes in the business environment (e.g. fashion).</li><li>The wholesaler may provide information on the product for the retailer.</li><li>Retailers do not have to pay for expensive storage facilities to hold inventory as they can buy smaller quantities compared to sourcing directly from the manufacturer.</li></ul>	<ul><li>The manufacturer loses control over what happens to the product after they have sold it and may not like the way the product is being portrayed by wholesalers or retailers.</li><li>There is less profit for the manufacturer as they have not sold directly to the customer.</li><li>Loyalty and any associated benefits of this (e.g. discounts) with the manufacturer cannot be gained.</li></ul>

5. **Benefits**
   - Retailer decides on price.
   - Retailer decides how to display product.
   - Retailers stock a range of products.
   - Retailers can offer extra services, e.g. credit facilities and deliveries.
   - Retailers can take advantage of buying in bulk.

Costs
   - Product might face competition from other manufacturers.
   - Extra financial costs associated with using a retailer.

6.

Supermarkets	Often very large organisations that buy large quantities and then sell them in their stores.
Discount retailer	They tend to provide non-branded products at a cheap price.
E-tailer	Shopping online and having the product delivered to you (e.g. through Amazon).
Convenience retailer	Often referred to as the corner shop. This type of retailer normally has a small shop where a limited number of products can be bought.

7. Examples will vary.

8. A system of warehouses and transport to get the product from the manufacturer to the customer.

9. See page 91.

10. See page 91.

PAGE 95

1. Above the line – mass media promotions.

Below the line – promotions to focused groups of people.

2. Into the pipeline – promotions to encourage retailers to stock products.

Out of the pipeline – promotions to encourage customers to buy from a retailer.

3. Above the line – newspaper advertising, radio advertising, billboards, internet websites, celebrity endorsement (NB make sure you describe each one).

Below the line – special offers/sales promotions, PR activities.

4. Depends on answer chosen in Q3. May require revision from National 5.

5. Into the pipeline – point of sale materials, sale or return, staff training, dealer loaders.

Out of the pipeline – free samples, loyalty schemes, vouchers, special offers.

6. Depends on answer chosen in Q5.

7. Attempts to improve the relationship and communication between the public and an organisation.

8.

Press releases	A press release is usually a written statement to the press (e.g. newspapers and TV stations) that communicates activities within the organisation.
Sponsorships	Organisations may sponsor events where there is likely to be a lot of public attention. Sport and charity events are often sponsored by large organisations that have their company name displayed on material that the sport or charity is distributing. Football strips sponsored by companies are a good example.
Charity donations	Organisations may donate sums of money to charities in the hope of not only helping a good cause, but also being seen as socially responsible. This will raise awareness of the organisation.

9.
- Websites for internet advertising.
- Social media for interacting with customers and analysing analytics for evaluating advertising success.
- E-mail for mailshots.
- Use of special offer websites to promote products (e.g. Groupon).

Chapter 4: Management of Operations

1. • Quality of raw materials.
   • Lead time.
   • Quantity of raw materials.
   • Location of supplier.
   • Reliability and reputation of supplier.
   • Storage space available.

2. • Ensure inventory is readily available at any one time.
   • Ensure production continues.
   • Avoid delays to customer orders.
   • Ensure over-stocking does not take place, which results in higher costs.
   • Avoid inventory deteriorating (e.g. fresh food) and/or becoming obsolete.

3. • Increased financial costs (e.g. storage, security and insurance).
   • Inventory could go to waste or deteriorate, resulting in inventory that needs to be discarded.
   • Higher risk of inventory being stolen.

4. • Production could stop and therefore employees and machines could be sitting idle.
   • Customers might not receive their orders on time, which could result in complaints.
   • The business could gain a poor reputation and image.

5. • **Maximum inventory level** – the highest amount of inventory that can be stored at one time. At this level, inventory costs will be at the minimum per unit because the organisation is at full capacity.
   • **Minimum inventory level** – the lowest amount of inventory that should be stored at one time. At this level, there is a danger that inventory levels could be too low and production could stop.
   • **Re-order level** – the quantity at which more inventory is ordered.
   • **Re-order quantity** – the quantity of inventory that has to be ordered to bring levels back to the maximum inventory level.
   • **Lead time** – the time that passes between ordering inventory and it arriving.
   See diagram on page 101

6. • **Centralised storage** – storing inventory in one place.
   • **Decentralised storage** – storing inventory in more than one place.

7. Just in time (JIT) is a method of inventory control that keeps cost levels to the minimum. As the name suggests, inventory arrives *just in time* for it to be used in the production process and goods are only manufactured when a customer order is received.

8. **Benefits**
   • Less cash is tied up in inventory.
   • Less storage and warehouse space is required.
   • Wastage should be reduced as only inventory required is ordered.
   • Changes in the external environment (e.g. fashion trends) will have a reduced impact.

Costs

- Suppliers who are reliable are required so that inventory is delivered on time.
- Production can stop if inventory is not delivered when required.
- Less environmentally friendly as more journeys with less inventory will be made.
- Delivery costs might be higher due to more journeys.
- Discounts for bulk buying (economies of scale) might be lost.

9. A warehouse is the name given to the place where finished products are held until they are ready to be distributed to the customer.

10. A system of warehouses and transport to get the product from the manufacturer to the customer.

11. • Reliability of other organisations.
    • Legal restrictions.
    • Availability of finance.
    • The product being distributed.
    • The image associated with the product.
    • The inventory management system being used.
    • The distribution capability of the manufacturer.

PAGE 108

1. **Job production** is when one product is made from start to finish before another one is made. The product is made to the customer's own requirements and this results in a unique or one-off product being made. Products made by job production are usually made by hand by someone who is very skilled at what they are doing.

   Batch production is when one group of identical products is made at any one time. All products in the batch move onto the next stage of production at the same time. Machinery and equipment can be cleaned and/or changed between batches to produce a different product. Batch production is often used when manufacturing a product that comes in different varieties, styles or sizes.

   Flow production (sometimes known as line production) is when parts are added to the product as it moves along the production line. The final product will have been made by the time it reaches the end of the production line. Flow production is sometimes called line production.

2. • Job production – wedding cakes, handmade chocolates, pieces of art, sandwiches made to order in a sandwich shop.
   • Batch production – cakes, newspapers/magazines, bread.
   • Flow production – cars/vans, computers and other electrical items.

3. See pages 105–106.

4. Labour intensive – use of employees in production.

   Capital intensive – use of machinery in production.

5.

Benefits	Costs
• Employees can use their initiative when required. • There is always a supply of labour available (though highly skilled employees might be more difficult to source). • Cheaper than purchasing and maintaining equipment.	• It costs money to recruit, select and train new employees. • The accuracy and the quality of work from person to person can vary.

6.

Benefits	Costs
• Machines can work 24/7 without the need for breaks. • Machines can produce a consistent and standardised accuracy and quality of work.	• Individual customer requirements cannot be met. • Breakdowns can occur, which can be expensive. • Employees become tired and bored of repetitive tasks that might need to be carried out.

7. Mechanisation means that there is some capital as well as some labour involved in production, e.g. people working machines.

8. Automation means that capital has replaced the need for humans to carry out the work required because machines, equipment and technology can do it instead.

PAGE 116

1. • Quality management – a total commitment towards quality from the organisation and its employees. Aims for perfection every time.
   • Benchmarking – comparing a product against the best in the market and trying to match this standard.
   • Mystery shopping – a person who makes a visit to a shop, buys something and then feeds back to the organisation. Employees won't know who the mystery shopper is.
   • Quality symbol – an award given to an organisation when it meets a particular specification or set of criteria. The symbol will usually appear on the product.

2. • Quality control – cheaper than other methods.
   • Quality assurance – faults can be discovered before the product reaches the end of the production process.
   • Quality management – a total commitment towards quality from everyone in the organisation, aiming to be the best.
   • Benchmarking – allows the organisation to be competitive.
   • Mystery shopping – unknown shopper so they will experience the shop and its customer service first hand. Accurate representation.
   • Quality symbol – recognised symbol awarded.

3. • Suppliers have produced or obtained their raw materials in an ethical manner.
   • The fair trade symbol that is on fair trade products means that those who have produced the product (e.g. farmers) have received a fair price for their product.
   • The supplier will treat their employees fairly and will have a commitment towards their welfare and health & safety.
   • The fair trade symbol is owned by Fairtrade International and is an independent assurance that the organisation is adopting a fair trade approach to business.

4. Recycling, being sustainable, minimise packaging, preventing pollution, using renewable energy sources, energy saving strategies

5. See pages 111–113.

6. • CAD – computer-aided design – used in the research and design stage of a new product before it is manufactured.
   • CAM – computer-aided manufacture – involves using computer-controlled equipment and robots in the manufacturing of a product (ie automation).

7. • Computer facilities (e.g. computer and internet) could be used for purchasing materials online.
   • E-mail can be used to confirm an order has been received and to let the customer know about the progress and status of the order (e.g. when it has been dispatched).
   • Websites could be used to compare the prices of different suppliers before deciding which one to purchase.
   • Deliveries could be tracked and traced via logistical companies' websites.
   • Computer programs (e.g. a database or spreadsheet) could be used to store inventory levels.
   • EPOS can provide automatic updates on inventory and sales levels.
   • Computer-aided design (CAD) can be used in the research and design stage of a new product before it is manufactured.
   • Computer-aided manufacture (CAM) involves using computer-controlled equipment and robots in the manufacturing of a product (ie automation).

Chapter 5: Management of People

PAGE 121

1. To ensure the organisation has the correct employees in place at the right time to meet organisational needs.

2. • The correct number of employees will be available at the right time who have the appropriate skills.
    • Future staffing levels/requirements will be considered.
    • Changes in the labour market will have been considered.

3. Internal recruitment is recruiting existing staff from within the organisation whereas external recruitment is recruiting staff who don't already work for the organisation.

4.

Benefits	Costs
• Job vacancy can be filled quickly, which means the time can be spent on other activities. • Employees are already known by the organisation and, if chosen, will have been so because they have demonstrated they have the ability to do the job. • Employees feel more valued and can become more motivated and productive if given the chance of promotion. • Money can be saved on advertising a job, recruiting, selecting and training, therefore increasing profitability. • Existing employees are already familiar with the policies, procedures and culture within the organisation and therefore do not need to be given guidance on this.	• The opportunity to gain new ideas from a new employee is lost and this could mean that new solutions to problems are not discovered. • An existing employee with the correct skills or ability for the job might not be available, therefore the position may remain unfilled. • There might not be that many existing employees that can apply for the position; therefore, limited candidates to choose from. • If a candidate is recruited internally, this will consequentially create another vacancy within the organisation that then needs to be filled (costly and time consuming). • Conflict amongst existing employees competing for the job might exist and this might cause poor working relationships.

5.

Benefits	Costs
• People with new ideas can be brought into the organisation that can help enhance the effectiveness of the organisation. • Can attract large quantities of applicants so that the organisation has a range of people to choose from (however, this could be a disadvantage as it will be more time consuming to look at large quantities of applications). • Job vacancies can be filled quickly using the help of recruitment agencies, meaning quicker productivity from the new employee. • Avoids conflict that may arise between competing employees within an organisation if only internal recruitment is used, therefore, better working relationships. • Specialist newspapers, magazines and agencies can be used to find appropriate staff, for example, for specialist posts meaning the most suitably qualified people can be targeted.	• Existing employees who apply but do not get the job may feel unvalued and therefore lose the motivation to work hard. • It can be expensive to advertise a job externally, for example, in a national newspaper and is usually a more expensive form of recruitment compared to internal. • May require a more thorough selection process, which can be expensive and time consuming, compared to internal recruitment. • There is always a chance that the wrong person is chosen as they are unknown to the organisation, despite employing a number of selection methods, which could be costly.

6. Newspapers/magazines, recruitment agencies, universities and colleges, recruitment websites, e.g. s1jobs

7.
- Internal vacancies could be circulated via e-mail or on the organisation's intranet.
- Application forms could be completed online.
- Databases could be populated with the details of people applying, which can be used as part of a mail merge when letters are being sent out.
- Websites could be used to advertise vacancies.

PAGE 125

1.
- CV – curriculum vitae, document created by an applicant that contains the information they want to disclose, e.g. education, employment history.
- Application form – document created by the organisation that asks questions of the applicant.
- Reference – a report from a previous employer or school/college.

2.
- They allow the organisation to meet applicants, ask them questions and to find out whether or not they are suitable for the job vacancy.
- They also allow the applicant to ask questions to see whether or not the vacancy is for them.

3.

Benefits	Costs
• Personality and appearance of the applicant is seen so that the organisation can see if they will fit in. • The content of the applicant's CV or application form can be checked, which means they can be sure the information is accurate. • The applicant can ask questions to make sure the job is right for them.	• Time consuming to carry out, therefore expensive. • Some people don't perform well at interviews, but might be suitable for the job, so the wrong person could be chosen. • Interviewer bias can exist, which means the most suitably qualified person might not necessarily be selected.

4. **One-to-one interviews**

One interviewer interviews all of the short-listed applicants and then makes a decision on who to select.

Successive interviews

Several interviewers interview each applicant separately.

Panel interviews

A panel interview involves one applicant being interviewed by several people at one time.

5.
- Skills and abilities can be confirmed.
- Confirmation of what the applicant has said on their application form can be obtained.

6. Any four from the table on page 121.

7. Assessment centres allow an organisation to see a large number of applicants undertaking a variety of tasks in different situations and realistic work-related scenarios.

8. **Benefits**

- Large number of applicants can be seen.
- Different things can be tested, e.g. team working.
- Can see how well applicants work under pressure.
- Interviewer bias is reduced.

Costs

- Expensive to carry out.
- Requires significant prior preparation.
- Facilities are required to hold the assessment centre.
- Several members of staff are needed to conduct the assessment centre.

PAGE 127

1. On-the-job training is training in the workplace whereas off-the-job training is training outwith the workplace, e.g. at a college or training provider.

2. Induction training introduces new members of staff to the organisation and its policies/procedures.

3. Continuing professional development – opportunities to develop as individuals and employees.

4. **Benefits**

- Jobs can be carried out better.
- Allows customer service to be better.
- Helps to achieve organisational objectives.
- Keep up to date with the external business environment.
- Contributes to the Scottish Government's life-long learning agenda.
- Record of training and development kept.

Costs

- Training is expensive.
- Time consuming to participate in development and training activities.
- Productivity is lower when training is being carried out.

5. Virtual learning environment – password-protected website that people can access to obtain training materials.

6. Saves on printing costs and is more environmentally friendly than providing hard copies of training materials. People do not need to travel to participate in training – less pollution.

7.

Benefits	Costs
• Can be accessed at any time of the day in any location. • Large numbers of people can access it. • Can be updated easily with notes, tasks, videos and other materials. • Interaction between users can take place through discussion forums and live chat facilities.	• People need to be self-disciplined to access the facility and carry out the activities. • People may prefer face-to-face contact rather than virtual learning; might not suit their own learning style. • Might be expensive to employ a specialist to set up and maintain a virtual learning facility.

8. To confirm that the person has achieved a certain standard on a work-based qualification.

9.

Benefits	Costs
• A recognised qualification can be gained. • Training often takes place on the job. • Assessment is carried out by a qualified Assessor. • The organisation benefits from having skilled staff.	• Time consuming to complete. • Some people might not want to complete a qualification. • Costs money to enter someone for a qualification.

10. Someone learns a trade on the job, e.g. joinery, and may attend a local college to gain a recognised qualification.

PAGE 131

1. Any three from the table on page 128.

2. Motivation theories can be used to understand what motivates people and can be applied in an organisation to motivate people.

3. • Maslow suggested that there are five levels of human needs that can be satisfied.
   • Each level needs to be satisfied before someone can progress to the next level, starting at the bottom of the pyramid.
   • If something is not satisfied at one level, they cannot progress to the next.

4. Theory X managers believe employees do not like work and try to avoid it, whereas Theory Y managers believe people achieve satisfaction from a job.

5. • Autocratic – authority and power rests with the leader and decisions are made by them.
   • Democratic – consultation and communication with employees is important.
   • Laissez-faire – no control is exercised over employees and people are left to get on with things themselves.

6. Autocratic

   • Benefits: standardised decisions across the organisation, tight control, quicker decision-making.
   • Costs: no opportunities to gain ideas from individuals, lack of opportunities for people to learn.

Democratic

   • Benefits: more opportunities to gain ideas, more opportunities to learn and participate, which can be motivating.
   • Costs: lack of standardisation, slower decision-making.

Laissez-faire

- Benefits: people are free to get on with things, people can feel empowered.
- Costs: lack of standardisation, limited achievement of organisational goals, support/ guidance only given when requested.

PAGE 137

1.
   - Staff turnover (the number of people leaving the organisation) will decrease, which will reduce costs associated with recruitment, selection, training and development.
   - The number of days staff are absent will reduce, which means productivity will be higher and more customer needs can be satisfied.
   - Employees will be more motivated and happier at work, which will result in customers receiving a better standard of service that will encourage them to return and also to provide positive feedback about the organisation.
   - Employees will be more willing to accept and adapt to any changes in the organisation as a result of the changing business environment; this will make implementing decisions easier as staff are not resistant to them.

2.
   - Staff turnover will increase, which will cost the organisation money to find replacements.
   - Absence rates will increase, resulting in lower productivity.
   - Employees will be less motivated, resulting in poor customer service.
   - Change in the organisation might be harder to implement, meaning decisions take longer to implement.

3. Trade unions represent the views of employees on different employment-related matters.

4. A works council is formed with representatives from across the organisation. It has the ability to access various types of information that relate to the organisation and it has the authority to take part alongside management in making decisions that relate to the workforce.

5.
   - There has been an increase in employment opportunities in the tertiary and quaternary sector at the same time as a decrease in the primary and secondary sector.
   - More people are becoming employed on part-time and temporary contracts compared to full-time or permanent ones to meet the needs of organisations that have to operate in a changing business and economic environment.
   - More women are now in employment in both full-time and part-time jobs and there has also been an increase in the number of women who have management positions.
   - Developments in technology have allowed more people to work out of the office, either as homeworkers or teleworkers.
   - The Government has encouraged people to become enterprising and as a result people are opting to become self-employed.
   - There has been an increase in the number of small businesses opening up because of the increase in people starting their own business.

6. **Benefits**
   - The organisation can recruit a wider range of employees.
   - Employees will be more motivated and therefore productivity will be higher.

Costs

- Could be costly to implement lots of different types of flexible working practices.
- May not always be possible to meet everyone's needs at the same time as the organisation's.

7. • Hot-desking – sharing a desk with others, booked when needed.
   - Teleworking – working outwith the organisation using technology to communicate.
   - Job-share – a full-time job is shared between two people.
   - Annualised hours – working a certain number of hours over the whole year, rather than a specific amount per day or week.
   - Flexitime – the employee has flexibility in their start and finish time but must usually work specific 'core hours'.

8.

Strike	Employees refuse to enter the workplace. They might have a picket line or demonstration outside the business to raise awareness of the issues they are facing.
Work to rule	Employees only carry out the tasks and duties written in their job description and no other tasks are performed.
Sit in	Employees refuse to work and 'sit in' the workplace.
Go slow	Employees work slower than normal in order to reduce productivity.
Overtime ban	No hours above the minimum required (as per the employee's contract) are worked.
Boycott	Employees refuse to carry out a new task or to use a new piece of machinery.
Demonstration	A gathering of people raising awareness of a particular issue.

9. A job no longer exists.

10. An employee complaint regarding a work-related issue.

11. • Complaint needs to be investigated by following the organisation's grievance procedure.
    - May have to consult Acas.
    - Motivation might be lower until issue is resolved.

12. An independent organisation that specialises in resolving disputes and disagreements between employees and their employer.

13.

Benefits	Costs
• Employees who have the potential for promotion can be identified, which can be motivating for them. • Feedback is given to the employee by their line manager to improve their work; praise can be given for work done well – this is motivating. • Can be a motivating experience if the appraisal is positive, which increases productivity. • Opportunities for CPD and training can be identified, meaning people can do their jobs better. • Targets for future performance can be discussed and agreed so that the employee has something to work towards.	• Some employees might see the appraisal as a 'tick-box' exercise and not take it seriously or commit to it, therefore wasting time. • Can be a demotivating experience if the appraisal is negative, therefore productivity decreases. • It is a time-consuming process to carry out; other activities are not being completed when an appraisal meeting is taking place and it is therefore costly and productivity decreases. • An employee might have too many development needs, which could result in additional stress for them and an increased workload.

14. • **Peer-to-peer appraisal** – when a colleague at the same level of the hierarchy conducts the appraisal.
   • **360 degree appraisal** – when the skills and performance of an employee are compared against others who work around them using a thorough self-evaluation process.
   • **Informal appraisal** – no formal structure is followed; instead a chat between employee and employer is had.

Chapter 6: Management of Finance

PAGE 146

1. The role of the finance department in an organisation is to:

Control costs and expenses

Costs and expenses must be controlled to avoid financial problems and the need to borrow money to cover these costs. Where necessary, management might have to take action to reduce costs and the amount of money going out of the organisation.

Monitor cash flow going in and out of the business

Money coming into the organisation and going out of the organisation needs to be monitored. There needs to be enough 'cash' available to be able to pay suppliers, trade payables and employees' wages. Making profit and having a good cash flow are two different things.

Forecast what might happen in the future

Preparing budgets and looking at past financial statements can help to identify trends and to see what might happen in the future. Action can be taken if necessary to avoid financial problems.

Monitor performance

Financial information can be used to compare one year against a previous year to see if performance has improved. This is useful to see if action taken in the past has worked and, where necessary, to take action in the future. Ratio analysis can be used to help monitor performance.

Provide information for decision-making

We already know that managers make lots of decisions. Financial information plays a crucial role in their decision-making and will often influence which course of action is taken.

2. See the table on page 144.

3. • How motivated staff are.
• The impact of external factors.
• How successful the business has been in increasing market share.
• The stage of the product life cycle.

4. Issue additional shares

Limited companies could issue extra shares to new or existing shareholders. Plcs can sell their shares on the stock market.

Leasing

Leasing means to rent. Businesses could rent equipment or premises rather than buying these outright.

Venture capitalists (or business angels)

Venture capitalists provide large loans to organisations that a bank or other lender may feel are too risky. They usually part-own the organisation in return for taking the risk.

5. See the tables on pages 145–146.

PAGE 151

1. To forecast the amount of money expected to be received or paid out over a period of time.

2. • To show if the business will have a surplus (more cash expected to come in than go out) or deficit (more cash expected to go out than come in) so that action can be taken to manage cash flow.
   • It can show if additional finance is required to ensure the business continues to operate effectively.
   • It can help control expenses by highlighting periods when expenses could be high; therefore, making sure the business has necessary money available to cover these.
   • Can help in making decisions; for example, whether to launch a new product, so that the organisation makes the best decisions it can.

3. • Bills cannot be paid.
   • A poor image might be given to suppliers and other trade payables.
   • Decisions cannot be made.
   • Objectives might not be achieved.

4. See the table on page 147 for methods and justifications.

PAGE 157

1. This shows a summary of the money that has came in and gone out of the organisation over the past financial year.

2. The statement of financial position shows the value (worth) of an organisation at a particular point in time. It shows what the organisation owns (assets) and what debts (liabilities) it has.

3. Gross profit – profit after buying and selling.

   Profit for the year – profit after other income has been added to gross profit and expenses deducted.

   Trade receivables – people who owe the organisation money.

   Trade payables – people whom the organisation owes money.

   Working capital – how easily an organisation can pay its short-term debts.

   Dividends – payments to shareholders for having shares in a company.

4. Bank, closing inventory, trade receivables, cash

5. Trade payables, bank overdraft

6. Wages, rent, electricity, advertising, insurance, rates

7. Through selling shares on the stock market.

8.
   - Spreadsheets could be used to store details of expenses and to create different financial statements.
   - Spreadsheets could be used to create graphs to show sales figures in different branches/ stores.
   - Specialist packages, for example, e.g. SAGE accounting, could be used to record financial transactions.
   - Mobile banking apps can be used to monitor funds and transfer money to suppliers.
   - PowerPoint presentations could be used to display profit figures at a meeting.
   - Skype could be used to hold a meeting between finance managers in different locations.
   - E-mail could be used to send invoices and statements to customers.
   - The internet could be used to find out share prices.